# poetry organic

*For Linda*
*Namaste*
*Clifton 4/15*

## Clifton King

*poetry organic*

*ISBN 978-0-9786935-2-7*

*Library of Congress Control Number: 2015936173*

*Cover art by author: Normandy countryside, France*

Many poems in this collection were first published, some in different versions, in the following literary journals, anthologies and websites: *Hummingbird Review, Magee Park Poets Anthology, Fullmoon, Blindmans Rainbow, Cranial Tempest, Wings, Wellspring Journal, Brother Jonathan Review, Barbaric Yawp, Expressions, RaodsPoetry.com, San Diego Family Magazine, CowboyPoetry.com, Poetalk, Small Brushes, Tidepools, San Diego Poetry Annual, Phantom Seed;* and in one previous collection: *Stolen Afternoons* (Royale Road Publishing 2006).

Excerpts from *Chicago*, and *Fog*, by Carl Sandburg, reprinted with permission of Harcourt Publishers.

*Printed in the United States of America.*

*Royale Road Publishing*

*for Katie Rose: my friend, my lover, my wife*

*Unless you love someone,*
*nothing else makes any sense.*
*e.e. cummings*

# Contents

# Giverny Garden

The garden is raucous with yellow and orange.
I find a bench in the shade.
Gravel pathways crunch beneath the crush of tourists.
A muted mix of Italian, French, that proper King's English,
and the American version, fills fragrance laden air.
Bees and butterflies are overwhelmed with choices.

Nearby, a woman talks on her cell phone in French.
Her words, music I don't understand.
In the distance, school children play, raise a bouquet of laughter.
A girl, voice so soft I barely hear her request,
asks that I take her picture.

I intended to write a poem, share this garden with you, the reader.
Perhaps even mention Monet's house and beloved lily pond
just across the road, beyond those green garden gates.
But, I see my lady coming down the path, sunlight in her hair.
She is the only poetry that interests me at the moment.
I will tell you about the garden later.

# Monet's Lily Pond

She claims that in a past life
she was a blossom in Monet's lily pond.
There, she basked in his pensive gaze
pleasured by silent brush strokes
as he redefined nature's images.

Today, clouds float among these lily pads
and pink petals, motionless in a mirrored sky.
*It must have been like this*
*on his last day*, I say.
*Quiet*, she says, *these flowers don't know.*
*See how they wait for him—open,*
*bright as a child's face.*

# Omaha Beach
## Normandy

today
there is no blood in the sea
no fallen soldiers on the beach
no sniper fire
no incoming rounds
  from battleships
  parked miles off shore
no landing crafts
  overturned in the surf
no enemy machine gun fire
  piercing the air
no cries of *Medic*
no young lives
  seeping into the sand

I cup my hands
raise the cold Atlantic
  to my lips
taste the salt
  of a nation's tears

## San Francisco Bus Ride

Across the aisle from us,
a big man, shirt open,
his bare belly like a ripe melon
in his lap; his hair wild, tangled
from San Francisco wind & neglect;
traces of his last meal in his beard;
a constant cascade of obscenities
from sun blistered lips.

He reaches out,
taps a Chinese woman on the arm,
shouts something
about the Pope & the President.
The woman refuses eye contact.
Boarding passengers
go to the back of the bus & stand.
Those two empty seats next to him
crowded with demons.

# Finding Chicago

I wanted to write poetry like Carl Sandburg.
I wanted to write about big cities and small towns,
about open prairies and rivers in the sky.
I wanted to write about the people:
plumbers, politicians, poets,
yet I'd never been east of Tucson.
So I quit my dead end job,
closed my savings account, all six-hundred dollars,
and went to Chicago in search of a poem.

*Chicago—City of the Big Shoulders,* wrote Sandburg.
But I couldn't find it.
I found Chicago falling down around an old black man
leaning on his battered bass case, the way you lean
on a friend when you're in need. And Thomas Jefferson
Brown was a man in need, shoulders sagging under
the weight of six decades of back alley blues bars
and his thirst for blended whiskey.

*Chicago—Player with Railroads and the Nation's Freight Handler,*
wrote Sandburg.
But I couldn't find it.
I found Chicago in a rusted heap of railroad cars, twisted
tracks and 55 gallon drums where bums built their fires.
Factories and warehouses empty, workers sitting in nearby
bars drinking beer, expecting checks at the end of the week.

*Chicago—Stormy, husky, brawling,* wrote Sandburg.
But I couldn't find it.
I found Chicago shimmering in the shadows of towering
concrete, steel and glass along 32nd Street, poets reading
in bookstores and coffee houses, children marching
to museums, women with slim hips in black silk gowns,
men in tuxedos and Italian shoes, dressed for the theater.

I wanted to write poetry like Sandburg.
But I couldn't find *his* Chicago.

# Underwear Sale

She calls from Macy's,
says there's a sale
& her daughter needs
new underwear
for her trip to Oregon.

I don't ask why,
afraid the answer might be
*too much information.*

I didn't buy new underwear
the last time I traveled to Oregon.
I know for a fact
many folks up there don't wear it.
Something about all the rain,
mold & mildew.

When we went to New York
I took my vintage boxers:
those Daffy Duck prints
& a couple pair of paisleys.

I don't believe I offended
a single New Yorker.
But then, what would?

When we flew to France
I packed my ancient underwear
right on top,
just for the TSA luggage inspector.

In Paris, the French scurried about,
baguettes under their arms,
cigarettes dangling from lips,
unconcerned
about my somewhat shabby shorts.

However, the gentleman in me
prevents any mention
of the new black lace panties
she packed for that trip.

New underwear:
I guess it's a girl thing.

## Organic

for Katie Rose

She floats in the placid pool
like a Monet water lily. I want
to harvest her beauty, keep
those star-like eyes in a safe place
only I know; somehow catch
her laugh mid-flight, place it
in my pocket where I can listen
to its music whenever I wish.

I ask if she would consider
being my woman, give up
her life as a single blossom.
*I might,* she says & swirls
away sending small ripples
across the pool & through
my heart. I ask her to dinner.
She tells me, *I eat only organic.*

I rush home, toss the McDonald's
bag & Big Mac box into the trash.

# Cruising the '55

I invite her into my fictitious '55 Chevy
for a cruise around the living room,
no plans to go any farther. Yet,

there is something in her laugh,
the way she touches my hand
and that look in her eyes

when she realizes I want her.
So, we drive down a different road,
travel back to those yester-years

of drive-in movies, the riddle
of how to finesse that first kiss
and that lurid call of the back seat.

# Home

Cirrus clouds curl in a rush
of Arizona sky. A desert breath
stirs forgotten wind chimes.

Quail scurry, scratch for seed,
ever cautious of the hawk.
But this is not my province,

so I journey the realm of memory.
There, she comes to me,
cold sea, blood of the earth,

endless glassy blue,
sprinkled with dolphin fins
and spouts that float, air so still.

# South of Sedona

Lost, in barren Arizona hills,
I stumble upon a ranch
this side of Cottonwood,
ask a woman for directions.

She, a Cherokee maiden
who wears feathers
in unruly locks, chants
a blessing for my safe
journey in this desolate
desert landscape: Indian
land, all myths and legend.

Here, sunsets compete
with foothills painted
the color of spilled blood;
parched waterholes harbor
spirits of the past; devil
winds speak to anyone
foolish enough to listen.

But, I have forgotten
her words, lost now
deep in the mystery
of her sun-browned face,
those eyes of fire
that shame shooting stars.

# Breakfast at the Deli
### with Billy Collins

If I had Billy Collins' appetite
I'd be foraging
for the poem hidden here.

Perhaps that young woman
behind the counter
who takes my breakfast order,
always that distant look
as if she can't get her lover
out of her mind.

Or those fry cooks,
battling for space on that huge griddle,
Spanish sound bites
peppered with, *Order up!*

Or the overwhelming aroma
of bacon & sausage grease
that clings to everything
like that stale cigarette smoke
in yesterday's bars.

Or that couple at the next table,
him with the look of an Iowa farmer
all doe-eyed at the big city;
her, in a pair of hip hugger Levis
showing off the back forty.

Yes, if I shared Billy Collins' tastes
I could toss these ingredients onto the page,
serve it up as a poem.

But then—
I'd be him. Come Monday morning
I'd have to ride that commuter train
into Brooklyn, spend the day lecturing
students who'd rather be someplace else.

Instead, I'm off to the beach where pelicans
skim wave tops, gulls argue over a sand crab,
and at the end of each day
                    the sun drowns itself in the sea.

# Breakout

Our terrier muscled his way
through the bedroom blinds,
pushed out the screen,
made his escape into the yard.

He jumped, no, levitated
up to that stretch of sacred ground
behind the retaining wall.

There, he squirmed
and bellied his way under
the old fence—and fled.

He roamed the neighborhood
not sure of his next move.
It was an impulse breakout,
no plan, no accomplice.

Search parties were launched.
The Pound was notified.
Police helicopters circled.

He was no ordinary escapee:
a bit of a nipper, but not a biter
unless you count the bloodied flesh
of our neighbor's buttock.

His crimes were minor:
misdemeanors more than felonies,
but he did have a bad attitude
and this wasn't his first offense.

Unbeknownst to all,
that big bosomed woman
down the street, familiar with
his habits, his canine tendencies,
took him in for the afternoon.

Later in the day he returned home,
head hung low, avoiding eye contact,
tail between his legs.

I built new fences, higher
with guard towers and razor wire.
I demanded punishment:
the minimum bread and water.

But, it's been suggested
it wasn't his fault, he may have
confinement issues, or a complex,
or flashbacks of days in the pound.

So, he's been placed on probation
if he agrees to get help.
Therapy begins tomorrow:
my session at 1:00; the dog's at 2:00.
We'll probably carpool.

# Double Overhead

*Waves are not measured in feet and inches,*
*they are measured in increments of fear.*
                                   Buzzy Trent


Somewhere, in a place as distant
as childhood, storms stir the sea.
Mountains of turquoise and cobalt
rise up like villains in a Grimm fairy tale.

On a morning so bright you forget
it is January, you paddle out
as you have a thousand times before.

Those first dark lines appear on the horizon:
furrows on the forehead of the world.

You race toward them, pray you find refuge
in deep water beyond towering crests,
that silent violence beneath their collapse.

Immortality rides the faces of these waves.
You believe in yourself, call it wisdom,
though from shore it looks like suicide.

You commit, let the sea swallow you
as you stretch a scar of your passage
across her swollen belly.

Life stampedes through your chest.
This is the way you want to die.

# In the Harbor

Afternoon wind sweeps in, a breath of sky that spawns sundered
waters, alters the face of this protected place. Reflected images
of schooners, sloops and sabots sink from sight, replaced with
sinuous pools of light. I sit topside, thin shadow of furled
mainsail cool on my face; sea air alive with the incessant,
insistent slap of halyards. Across the narrow finger of water,
a new owner of an old boat, inspects, rummages, discovers.
He finds a pair of oars laid across the bow. *Do I get a small boat
with these,* he laughs and tosses them aside. In that murky abyss
between us a sea lion ripples the surface: stout nose, whiskers
and huge black eyes. Then that long arc of her body that mimics
earth's curvature slips silent below. Sun low, shadows long,
I lock the hatch, take what I remember of the day with me.

## A Letter to Mother

Dear Mom,
I know we haven't talked for some time,
not since the night before your death.
And I'm sure you don't remember
my last words to you. In truth,
I can't recall them myself.

But then, does it really matter?
We all knew you hadn't heard a word
in days, only now and then uttering
sounds none of us could make out.

You died in the morning, while I slept,
finally surrendering to the lack of sustenance.
A decision we all made on your behalf.
A decision we have to live with.
A decision I question to this day.

I had no idea it would take so long.
The Doctor said it was because your heart
was so strong. Mom, I had no idea
the dieing would take so long.

Dad cried that morning, alone in his chair,
head bowed, as if in prayer.
But he never was a religious man.
Yet, it's times such as this that bring men
to God, and his mantra that morning:
*I was supposed to go first,*
*I—was supposed to go first.*

Mom, I couldn't watch when they came,
men in dark suits and somber faces,
to carry you away, a small bundle
on a stainless steel gurney.

Yet, even from my hiding place
in the tiny chapel I could hear the rattle
of steel wheels down the hall.

It's hard to believe it's been seven years
since that morning and my life has moved on,
changed: the separation, the divorce, a new woman,
and my new granddaughter. I wish you could see her
Mom. She has beautiful brown eyes
and a smile that's already breaking my heart.

And it probably won't come as a surprise
that Dad hasn't changed a thing in the house.
Those shells you collected in Mexico still fill
a basket on the bottom shelf, and the cookbooks
you cherished, their secrets shared so often,
now just gather dust in the bookcase.

Mom, maybe I shouldn't tell you
I still have your ashes. They're in that shiny
cardboard box I picked up at the funeral home.
I wanted Dad to scatter them across some slope
of desert ground where you two had camped;

someplace filled with sunshine and fingers
of shade tossed down by ancient saguaros;
someplace where you warmed yourself at night
near rocks blackened by eons of silent campfires,
stars so close it seemed you could touch them.

But Dad would have none of it.
He said he has those years of you two together
and doesn't want his final memory of you
to be a wisp of dust in the desert wind.

So Mom, I'll keep your ashes a while longer,
and someday return you both
to the place you loved—with the one you loved.

19

# A Bridge an Island Does Not Make...

    yet the inhabitants of Coronado
would have us believe otherwise.
Why else the Coronado bridge,
the Coronado ferry?

Even with all its manufactured charm
and outrageous real estate prices,
Coronado is not an island.
It is in fact a peninsula.
But Coronado Peninsula
just doesn't have the same ring.
Island says exclusive, expensive.
Peninsula says—well, I don't know
what it says, but it's obvious
Coronado doesn't want to say it.

I think it's time they faced the facts,
admit you can get there without
crossing a bridge or taking a ferry.
Maybe have the Chamber of Commerce
post directions on their website:

*Take I-5 south to Imperial Beach.*
*You'll know when you're there*
*by the stench of Tijuana's raw sewage*
*lapping at its shores. Drive west*
*along Palm Avenue, past the K-Mart,*
*Dairy Queen and Hector's Tamale Stand.*

*But if you don't want to spend sixty-seven dollars*
*for lunch, best stop there for a bite.*
*We don't allow fast food restaurants in Coronado.*

*And don't be intimidated by the hoards*
*of young Hispanic men, their shaved heads*
*and tattooed necks, those angry looks*
*they flash as you pass.*
*We don't allow them in Coronado either.*

*Head north out Silver Strand Blvd.*
*We're just a few miles up the road*
*past the Del Coronado, a dinosaur*
*of a tinder box waiting for that one*
*careless smoker, that single spark*
*from century old wiring. That's us*
*nestled against the Naval Air Station.*

*Don't worry about those frequent flights*
*of Navy planes strafing Coronado Beach.*
*With San Diego Airport*
*just across the bay you have to love*
*low flying aircraft to live in Coronado.*

Shouldn't that be *on* Coronado
if it's an Island? Hey, you say tomāto,
I say tomäto. But anyone who has
ever looked at a map will tell you,
        an island Coronado is not.

# Thursday Morning at Swami's

The concrete bench at Swami's
is cold, damp with dawn.
I sit, careful not to lean against
the bronze memorial plaque
imbedded in its back.

The sea is calm, air heavy
with scents of salt water,
fresh coffee and sunscreen.
Clouds the color of dirty laundry
threaten rain. A scattering of surfers
stare at the horizon. Meaningless swells
march to shore. A fishing boat loiters
out beyond the kelp beds where
a lone dolphin breaks the surface.

On the beach, ropes of rotting seaweed
lie tangled along last night's high tide line.
A swarm of women run at water's edge,
flash of pink shoes, bodies tan and taut.
Sweat glistened arms and legs announce
intentions of eternal youth. A rotund man
in a shirt wet with his efforts climbs
the 140 stairs from beach to parking lot
for the third time.

Down the sidewalk two young women,
girls really, push baby strollers.
Conversation is constant, animated,
a flurry of ringed fingers and bright nails.
One has purple highlighted hair,
a butterfly tattoo on her shoulder.

The other hides her face behind
a pair of enormous sunglasses.
A fire breathing dragon hugs her calf.
Enough red ink to stop traffic.
Beneath her blouse, a telltale baby bump.
As they pass she speaks to her friend,
*All I know is —*
*I'll never date a surfer again.*

# All My Tomorrows
### —for McKenna

If you were not on my mind at this moment,
I might notice those bananas, their thick fragrance,
brown spots telling me they are beyond ripe,
fit only for banana bread today, the garbage tomorrow.

If you were not on my mind at this moment,
I might push and poke at the couch cushions,
those hollows that resemble impressions sunbathers
leave in the sand. I might attempt to clear that clutter
off my dining room table: random stacks of poetry books,
small slips of paper peeking from between the pages;
my laptop and printer, a hushed hum linked
by that umbilical twist of copper cables.

If you were not on my mind, I might be annoyed
by that flood of sounds filling my open window:
that constant collision of waves against shore;
Harleys cruisin'101, their low erratic rumble echoing
in my bones; the neighbor, so near I hear the clink
of dinner dishes and that Johnny Cash CD
he plays every night.

Yet, I ignore these mundane moments because
you are on my mind, now and all my tomorrows.
That's what a new granddaughter does to a man.

# Storm Warning

A purple silhouette of Oceanside Pier,
that massive finger of Dana Point
conquer the horizon like an invading army.
Yet, the sea does not surrender, not to them,
nor those *Devil Winds* that sweep in
with their dry desert breath. Even the sailor
doesn't understand the whims of this woman,
how swiftly her mood morphs when winds
whisper secrets we cannot comprehend;
when sunlight, sudden as a lightning strike,
changes her into liquid chrome and she
lures the unwary far from safe shores.
So all who answer her call beware.
The sea can be as dangerous as a love affair.

# The Proposal

The old Hotel Del,
with its six-hundred-dollar-a-night rooms,
leans and creaks from a century long
attack of ocean breezes. The sky is cluttered
with clouds where the sun plays hide-n-seek.
A swarm of tourists parade down the sidewalk.
Sailboats skirt Point Loma, ghosts dancing on the sea.
Navy planes thunder above the sand, surprise beach goers.
We lie against a dune, the sun's radiance stored
in every grain of sand warm against our backs.
I have the ring, precious metal and gemstone.
I have the question in my heart, then in my mouth.
It flutters in the wind like a sparrow.
I so wanted it to fly like an eagle.
On the nearby shore waves raise a ruckus.
Yet, I hear only the music of your answer.

# Sunset Wedding

March 23, 2012

We gather in a friend's home
perched on a bluff above the Pacific.
There's the minister, his suit a formal flower
among the Hawaiian shirts and print dresses.
The requisite DJ plays a love song so familiar
we sing along, yet can't recall its name.
Guests fill their bellies with food and drink,
huddle in small groups of like-minded:
surfers, ladies from Yoga, the Friday lunch bunch.
The evening sun threatens to hide behind tufts
of fog scattered along the horizon and drag
our sunset wedding down like a sinking ship.
We cue the DJ and give the preacher a nod.
The sun disappears and reappears in the clouds
like a child playing peek-a-boo. Outside the window
a line of pelicans glides through our vows.
You say, *I do,* and I can't imagine my life without you.

## Wedding Vows
March 23, 2012

Katie Rose,

You are my sunrise,
my morning sky,
my sea breeze,
my sunlight,
my starlit nights,
the dawn of our new life together.

You are the rose in my garden,
the Rose of my life,
the reason for my next breath.

From this day forth
I promise to kiss and caress.
I promise to laugh with you,
cry with you, comfort you.
I promise honesty and respect.
I promise love.
I promise my heart to the person
you are: my friend, my lover.
I promise my heart to the person
you are soon to be—my wife.

# Dirty Dishes

They litter our kitchen counter
like homeless in a New York
subway station: unwashed,
memories of their last meal
swept away by new hunger.

A salad bowl catches my eye:
bits of romaine, a red sliver
of tomato deprived of dressing
huddle like lost orphans.

I see our wine glasses, recall
the way your lips invited
that magic elixir in, how
they formed a perfect O.

These remnants of foreplay
lie untouched, just as those
tangled sheets of our dessert
still embrace our unmade bed.

# Welcome to New York

Our first morning in New York
we eat breakfast at a little yogurt bar
in The Village: homemade granola,
organic yogurt, blueberries
& steaming mugs of apple spice tea.
Outside, wind that seems to come
from every direction demands
turned-up collars & clutched coats.
Sidewalks are littered
with a surging mosaic of fallen leaves.
We wander without purpose for hours.
Then, with a shopping trip to Soho
in mind, we fail repeatedly
in our attempts to hail a cab.
I stop a man wearing a stocking cap
pulled so low his eyes invisible.
He smells of tobacco & stale beer.
I ask the secret of getting a taxi.
*Haven't used one in years*, he says.
Yet, he still shares a few hints before
disappearing back into the sidewalk crowd.
Confident with my new found knowledge
I stand at the curb, hand raised.
I spot a cab, roof light lit.
Expectation sweeps over me,
like finding a motel vacancy sign
while traveling the interstate late.

Just across the intersection
the cabbie waits on a red light,
fidgety as a thoroughbred
in the starting gate. I try
to make eye contact, seal the deal.
Then, just as the light changes
a man in a business suit dashes
across the street, stops not ten feet
from where I stand & raises his hand.
Our cab crosses the intersection
& picks him up. As the taxi pulls away
he smiles at us from the back seat.

# A December Day at Warm Water Jetty
—for Jeff

Remnants of a waning moon
inch toward a ragged horizon
the sun still low in the east.
A whisper of breeze
lays a hint of texture
on this vast carpet of ocean.
Out beyond small swells
a flotilla of lobster buoys.
Nearby, the blue
fins of a snorkel fisherman
break the surface
and a lone pelican skims the sea.
Gulls rest on the jetty,
soon to resume their scavenger ways.
Down the beach
two children play in the sand.
Their mother stands at water's edge,
her red sweater like a lighthouse beacon.
A boy carrying a surfboard
runs toward the water, conjures up
thoughts of my old surf buddy Jeff.
For years we hunted waves
together along this beach:
years before the Doctors told him,
*There is nothing we can do;*
years before I watched his ashes
disappear into the blue abyss of the Pacific.
Now, when I paddle out
the water is so crowded with memories
I can scarcely tell today from yesterday.

# German Brown

Along the stream
a stand of birch, tall
against a frozen sky.

Crystal waters slow dance
between her banks.
The gentle cascade, music
painted across winter's face.

Beyond the shallows,
below rippled sunlight,
dark shadows reside.

# Along for the Ride
— ode to a '36 Oldsmobile

I was in love the summer of '59
for the second time. The year before
it was a girl whose face I can't recall.
But back then I wrote her name
on my blue canvas binder, in the margins
of text books, on the palm of my hand.
Then, she took up with a high school boy
from El Cajon and broke my heart.

But, being young and resilient
I found a new love. She was older
than I by nearly a decade, yet
satisfied something within me:
those raging hormones of automotive lust
every 15-year-old boy must confront.

My heart nearly stopped at the sight
of her flared fenders,
their swooping curves stamped
from the same steel as battleships;
torpedo like headlights
hung on the snout of a long hood.

I lusted after her spring steel bumpers,
and Herculean running boards
that could shoulder the weight
of my adolescent daydreams.

I was in love with her single taillight,
massive chrome door handles,
her hardwood door frames,
and the cold iron of a flathead six
I knew would fly me
down that highway of youth.

And I knew I was through with women.
The rattle of a loose muffler, squeak
of a fan belt and that whine
of a transmission low on lubricant
a much more pleasing prospect.

Then,
a cracked block ended the affair.
The cost of repair far surpassing
the outlay for dinner and a movie.

So it was in the summer of '59
I decided to give girls another try.
Now, five decades later,
      I'm still asking myself why.

## An Interview With Gary Snyder Resurrects My Brother

Reading *Morning Tea with Gary Snyder*
I come upon a reference to the Yuba River.
A swift current of memories sweeps me back
to the seventies, my late brother Robert.

He spent a decade on cobbled banks,
in her frigid waters, dredging for gold.
Spring and summer his tent leaned
with that persistent wind of the canyons.

Winters were, as Snyder said about
his barn office, "...too damn cold."
So, those windowless winter nights were
abandoned until spring's invitation.

One autumn morning they found Robert,
face down at the bottom of Redman Gorge.
What they didn't find was his dust or nuggets,
his rifle or that Colt .45 he always carried.

The casket was closed, the service short.
In the corner of Grass Valley Cemetery
a simple granite head stone reads:

> Robert King
> Beloved Son and Brother.

Graveside, a woman and small boy stood
silent. I asked, "Did you know Robert?"
A single tear fell on freshly turned earth
as she took the boys hand in hers.
> "Let's go Bobby. It's over."

# Boneyard

observations from a kayak

I paddle into the morning cold,
fog following the night into the west,
a breeze off the sea cool against my skin.
Yellow comes the sun
painted on a pale canvas of morning sky.
Its warmth: the embrace of an old friend,
                    a lover's kiss.

Somewhere, a storm licks at the sea,
pushes her away sending swells marching,
hundreds, thousands of miles
to rise up, then tumble and die.
The murmur of waves: words whispered
                that go straight to the heart.

Beyond the surf, a flotilla of kelp
heaving with the ebb, alive with shorebirds
and black eyed seals.
On the distant shore a train rumbles,
sounds a long blast, then falls silent.

Now —
            only the croak of a Cormorant,
            the tremolo call of the Loons
            and the water dripping off my paddle
            rippling the transparent world below.

# Lost Wedding Ring

She is sure that small circle of commitment
is hiding out in her purse, somewhere among
the lipstick & rouge & sunscreen, perhaps
attached to an old piece of chewed gum. Of course
she has searched that bottomless abyss before,
even found keys lost months ago. Yet, no sign
of that cherished gold band. Once again,
out of desperation, she upends that cavernous bag,
shakes it like one of those paint mixers at Home Depot.
Organic fruit pits, granola crumbs & unrecognizable
bits of unnamable substances litter the kitchen counter.
Alas, among the debris a sparkle, a shimmer, her ring.
She slips it on, holds it up to the light & muses,
*Hmmm, I remember the diamonds bigger.*

.

## Georgia Pines

I remember a small shack
in a dark corner of the Georgia woods,
walls made from apple boxes
and scrap lumber.
I still feel those hot summer nights
and warm rain the roof let in.

I remember Papa with his pipe.
The flare of wooden matches,
that bitter whiff of sulfur,
the sweet aroma of tobacco
mingled with the pungent
perfume of Georgia Pines.

I still hear the far off cry
of a train whistle in the night,
and Papa's stories
about ridin' the Macon Line.

I remember the night they came:
the torches; the shouting;
the rope with its ugly knot,
noose pulled wide enough
to swallow a man.

I'll never forget that toss of rope
over the limb of a Georgia Pine,
men struggling with Papa,
the snap of rope pulled taut,
the grunts and squeals,
the kicking,
the silence,
and Papa's shoe on the ground.

## La Jolla Cove

We reach into summer
from these last days of December
& journey placid waters,

drift through kelp beds
rising from the green broth,
& surrender to the ebb.

From a tangle of brown leaves
wide eyed seals
question our intentions.

Caves & craggy points
below crumbling bluffs
testify to the rage of wind & sea.

We linger
near the edge of humanity,
the masses within sight.

Reluctant to return
we wait for that silence
of heaven's half-light.

# Woman in the Pool

I first saw her, chin deep
in the pool. A floppy brimmed
beach hat hid her face,
shaded glacier blue eyes.

A lotus blossom came to mind.
Red. All heart and compassion
if you believe the Buddhists.

Her body, the slender stalk
that anchored her, swayed
and curved beneath the surface.

She rekindled my desire
for the feminine flower.

Now, my garden blooms
with African Iris, Lavender
and a single perfect Rose.

## On Viewing an AK-47
## in an Art Gallery

You are not beautiful, exactly,
hanging on the wall in ironic silence,
pointed skyward as if in the hand
of a jubilant freedom fighter,
the last enemy dead at his feet,
the people free—for the moment.
In truth, you are merely rusted
bones of a decaying memory.
Exposed, your reason for being
crumbles like the poorly mixed
                 cement of society.

We've all seen you, or your kind,
in Vietnam, the deserts of Iraq,
the foothills of Afghanistan. But now,
you live on our city streets, consort
with gangbangers in black Escalades,
do-rags and three-hundred-dollar Nikes.
Children lie in morgues, and cities die
as your bullets shatter night air where
blood puddles on neighborhood sidewalks.
You are not beautiful.

# Rebuilding the Entry Gate

Men march around like ants at a picnic.
Each carries his bread crumb:
a piece of rebar, a coil of electrical cable,
a length of lumber. At first glance
it seems an orchestrated effort,
as if that man perched on the tailgate
of an old rusted Ford pickup, plans
spread wide, coffee cup within easy reach,
has actually shared the secrets
of this project with the worker ants;
as if between those perpetual coffee breaks,
the multiple lunchtimes, those group
*stand and stare* sessions someone
actually knows what's going on.
Then you check the calendar.
These men have been milling around
since the Bush administration.
Many of the original crew are now retired.
Yet, nearby residents, the recipients
of early morning jack hammers,
a constant cacophony of power tools,
near fatal pedestrian access, should rejoice.
Remember, it took eighteen months
to build the Empire State Building.

# New York Taxi Ride

The cabby stands next to an ancient mini-van,
his yellow shirt damp with sweat; a white toothed grin
bright as last night's quarter moon. A blank stare
meets my request of, *The Village please.*
*The Village,* he says, more question than affirmation,
and confesses he's only been in New York a week,
fresh from Hattie, wife and four children still there.
The recent tsunami destroyed their home; his uncle,
swept out to sea, not seen since. Before we can hail
another cab, our luggage is tossed in atop a rusty
tire iron, a spare tire with not a trace of tread
and three quarts of forty weight Pennzoil.
We merge into rush hour traffic, his driving skills
innovative and somewhat frightening.
The cabby talks non-stop, looks at us in the rear view
mirror more than he watches the road. Outside,
New York sizzles in September heat. The cab is like
a sweat box in a yester-year French penal colony.
*Could you turn up the air?* I ask. Our cabby smiles.
*Yes, it be hot,* he says—and rolls down his window.

# A Letter to Tony Hoagland

### victim of a poetry workshop

Dear Mr. Hoagland, or may I call you Tony?
I wish to apologize for the recent gutting
of your poem *A Color of the Sky*.
But, it lay there on the table,
like a fresh caught sea bass,
twitching on about windy days,
apologies and the ocean,
one lifeless eye, still moist with hope,
reflecting sunlight like an August moon.
What else could we do but slit you
from metaphor to simile,
reach in, rip out every syllable,
sharpen our scalpels and dissect
each organ, each thought,
every line we couldn't comprehend?
However, we did find the flesh
of your work plump, rich
in the nutrients infant writers need.
So, we grilled it lightly,
passed it around, each taking a nibble
—just enough to inspire.

## Cowboy

The cowboy's gone you know. Oh, there's
still men raisin' cattle an' drivin' 'em to market.
But there're herdin' them steers with Jeeps,
an' ridin' fence in helicopters, then goin' home for supper.
An' they wear sunscreen an' Rayban sunglasses,
get Sundays off for church, an' a family Bar-B-Q.
They ain't cowboys. Not real cowboys.

An' there's city folk playin' at cowboyin'.
Anyone can do it, if 'n you got the money.
Jump a jet to Montana or Wyoming or Okalahoma,
slip into some tight britches an' a flannel shirt.
Don't forget the Stetson. Ride an' ol' swayback mare
behind a bunch a cows for an hour or so,
an' eat some bacon an' beans. Then schedule a massage
before the limo ride to the airport.
They surely ain't cowboys. Not real cowboys.

A cowboy sits a horse like he was born
in the saddle, leanin' into the Wyoming wind,
bandana high on his nose, hat pulled tight,
tipped into the dust churned by a thousand hooves.
His face, dark an' leathery from the Arizona sun,
eyes clear and truthful as winter air sweepin'
down through Colorado.

A cowboy walks like he's still in the saddle,
that silver jangle from his boots. He smells
of sweat an' wet horse flesh, an' chewin' tobacco.

A cowboy talks to his horse durin' the day,'
an' serenades the cattle at night, while sittin'
'round the campfire, boilin' coffee, an' watchin'
mesquite smoke mingle with the stars.

Yeah, the cowboy's gone—but his ghost rides
the Chisholm Trail, stirrin' up dust 'tween
Abilene an' Red River. An' he can be found
in most any cattle town from Cheyenne to
Wichita, Denver to Dodge.

So, if you're over that way, you may feel the ground
tremble, an' smell cattle an' horses an' men,
hear the squeak of leather on leather, saddles an' chaps,
an' rawhide ropes, an' the hollow beat of hooves.

An' if you wait 'till sundown, 'till the trail is black,
an' listen with a keen ear, you might hear the moans
of cattle an' the melody of cowboy ballads
in the lonesome prairie night—you might,
but you know—the cowboy's gone.

# The Quail Come Later

I sit in the shade, watch my father's slow steps,
listen to the click of his cane as he crosses the porch.

A long arc of seed floats from his hand,
dances in the gravel beneath a mulberry tree.

Mourning doves swoop from rooftops;
yellow breasted finches flutter from bare branches;
all aware of the red-tailed hawk circling above.

We sit together in the silence of the morning.
*The quail come later,* he says.

## Springtime

there is a place in our memories
a time of youth and yearning
when tomorrows were like seeds
buried in the warm earth
their blossoms yet unimagined

# Permissive

How many times
can I turn to the sea,
expect her to satisfy me;
watch a pelican's
silent flight across waves
wishing I could fly;
see the sun slip
behind the horizon
leaving a sky
that makes me
hold my breath?
And will I ever tire
of rainbows in wet sand
or the turning tide
calling my name?
For me, the sea is a lover
who never says no.

# Soul Searching

I spend the morning
in the graveyard
visiting old friends.

Fog inches its way
up the small valley,
lies against the hillside.

Granite headstones
stand in rows,
soldiers at attention.

I walk among the names,
grass thick
with weeks of neglect.

Morning dew,
tears from old memories,
saturate my feet.

I step over, around, the dead,
pause at a small stone marker.

> *ROY G. KING*
> *1890 — 1932*

Is this all that remains?
Is this all
   any of us can expect?

# Dress Code

It hangs in the back of my closet
cloistered in Hawaiian shirts and Levis.
Not a fitting end, some may say,
for a Brooks Brothers. What do you do
with a two-thousand-dollar suit,
fold it like the flag at a funeral,
hand it to the next of kin? Suits
have always been a mystery to me:
corporate uniforms not unlike
those orange jumpsuits worn
by county jail inmates. Executives
and felons alike, fresh from the mold
like a batch of gingerbread men.
Their only chance to be individuals:
that overpriced silk tie for corporate types;
a defiant prison tattoo for those in orange.
But lately, it's become more difficult
to distinguish one suit from the other.

# Beach Walk

I walk our favorite beach,
wish with each step
you were at my side.

A small chip from some far-off
mountain, massaged by the sea
for eons, lies half buried in the sand.

It sparkles like your eyes;
its shape similar to a heart.
I am no longer alone.

## Library Trip

There on the third shelf, standing like soldiers
at attention, travel books about Europe. I pull Paris
from the lineup. *A week in Frankfurt* leans left,
fills in the gap between France and Germany.
There is only one book on Spain. My love never
expressed a desire to visit Madrid or Barcelona.
I leave it on the shelf. I take Paris home with me,
unfold the maps, peruse hotel listings. I wonder
if making love in a French hotel will be all that different
than here, the Pacific whispering in the background. Yet,
the thought of her lying beside me, as Parisian sunlight
slips in beneath the shades, our only communication carnal,
drives me to the airline's website in search of flight schedules.

# Department Store Cowboy

I pull into the rodeo grounds, park behind a long line of rusty
pickups and horse trailers. And there she is, standing in the
middle of a bunch of bull riders waiting to hear who drew Black
Lightning or Twister, or that cream colored beast that broke poor
ol' Billy Watson's back last spring. She's slim and tan, like a
leather strap. Honey colored hair hangs down her back. Her Levis
fit the way men want women's clothes to fit, and I'm already
jealous of the horse she rides. I watch awhile, catch her eye,
flash a smile. But she's not interested in a guy in sandals and a
Hawaiian shirt, driving a van with a surfboard strapped up top.
So I make a trip to that western wear store over in the mall,
buy some Wrangler britches, a shirt with pearl snaps, a genuine
leather belt with a silver buckle the size of Kansas and a Stetson
hat that cost more than my first car. I borrow my brother's pickup
and three of his dogs, return to the rodeo grounds for my chance
at romance. I walk right up and say, *Howdy*, trying to force a
little Texas onto my California tongue. She looks me up and
down like maybe I'm the rodeo clown and says straight out,
*I need a bull ridin' man, and it's plain to see you ain't nothin'*
*but a department store cowboy.* It's over just that quick, don't
even get my eight seconds in the saddle. She's right you know,
chewing tobacco and bunkhouses just aren't my style. And I've
never tossed a bedroll over one of those fancy Mexican saddles.
Hell, I've never even been on a horse, and the only thing I know
about cows is that Von's has some of the better parts on sale now
and then. But I'm not giving up that easy. Nothing I want more
than to be her cowboy man. And if she won't settle for less, guess
I can make some changes, dump my stock portfolio, sell the
yacht, turn back the Beemer, 'cause a cowboy ain't nothin'
but poverty wearin' spurs an' a hat. She wants a cowboy,
I can do that. Because you know—
I got a real hankerin' to ride in that midnight rodeo.

## 87 rue Claude Monet

We wander the country roads of France, Paris
to Normandy, discover a small hotel in Giverny,
Monet's house and lily pond just down the road.
The innkeeper is a burly man with a tousle of hair
wild as the Jasmine that consumes the garden
wall out front. His English decent; our French
nonexistent. His wife is a wispy woman,
a sculptor who hammers and welds steel.
They welcome us with the warmth of old friends.

At dawn the village streets are silent,
that daily invasion of tourists still hours away.
We take our café au lait into the garden, the brick
pathway still damp from night air. A spider works
a web between long tendrils of blue lavender.
Tiny jewels of dew dance with her every move.
A bee investigates our steaming mugs. Beyond
ancient garden gates the rattle of a diesel,
perhaps a shopkeeper on his way to work.
We settle into wicker garden chairs. Somewhere,
a tea kettle demands attention. In an apple tree
redwings chatter a morning song. I wonder
if Monet ever painted this garden. I wonder how
I could love you more than I do at this moment.

# Reunion Meal

Years after Mother's death,
family sits around the kitchen table.
Old wooden chairs creak under us,
much like our own bodies. Father leans
his cane against the wall. Someone asks,
*Do you remember...?* and we all do.
*And what about the time...?* and we all laugh.
Father says, *Your mother and I....* and we all cry.
My sisters fix Mother's favorite dish:
spare ribs marinated in beer. As much for her,
I believe, as for us. I am asked to give the blessing
but can think only of asking God
to return Mother just for this one meal
so we can be the family we haven't
been for decades, be children again,
Mother alive with the hope of the future,
Father strong in youth. But the words will not
leave my mouth. So, I thank God for this day
and we push childhood to the back of our plates.
We share in Mother's favorite meal
and in Father's eyes, I catch her smiling.

# Life's Song

The day after his 87<sup>th</sup> birthday
I hear my father in the next room,
his restless sleep murmuring in the dark.
Those same sounds he makes while napping
in that big chair: an occasional catch
in his breathing; a stutter; the hesitation
of a body trying to remember what comes next,
tired from the years but not yet ready to rest.

He has come to witness the miracle
that is his newest great granddaughter:
her petite, perfect hands that grip his finger;
tiny toes that curl when he strokes the bottom
of her foot; that small sound of her breathing
while she sleeps as a new body learns.

Now, I listen to the staccato song
of my father's sleep and realize how similar
those sounds: a new body trying to learn life;
an old one, trying not to forget.

# Father's Fedora

Father died last year.
Nothing the paramedics could do.
The Doctor's attempts failed.

For three days he lingered
somewhere
between here and heaven.

Later,
I gave everything to Goodwill.

Yesterday I found his favorite hat
on a shelf in the closet.

But now,
without it perched atop his bald head,
a little cocked to the side
à la John Wayne;
without that glint in his eyes
warning of something to come;
without that easy laugh of his;

it's nothing
more than a handful of felt.

# The Hunt

1851—aboard the New Bedford
whaling ship *Benjamin Tucker*


I see the spout, white and ghostly
   like smoke from a signal fire
The very breath of life
   reveals you, betrays you
Do you see us running with the wind
   sails billowed, full, taut against the sky
Can you hear our bow slice the sea
   hear the mast creak and rigging sing
Do you know who we are
   this crew of thirty men and a boy
Do you know we have come
   to chase and slaughter

Will you run before we lower the boats
   or must we first kill your calf
To lure you, bring you near the men
   men eager for the hunt
Men with harpoons and coils of rope
   steel lances and fluke spades
Men with wives and children waiting
   men willing to face you for their share
Will you turn on them in their small boats
   spill them into the sea to die
Will you scream when the harpoon
   rips into your flesh
Then dive and run for the depths
   streaming blood behind
Or let us pull you along side
   and plunge a lance into your heart

Will you cry when the sea runs red
  and you spout blood with every breath
When the end comes, the flurry
  that violent thrashing
And you beat the water with your tail
  and with a final shudder
  roll over on your back
We will slice you into strips
  render your flesh and bones
And the sea will be a pool of blood
  thick and stinking
And we will store you in the hold
  every butchered piece
And you will become
  oil for our lamps
  corset stays for our ladies

Did you imagine you would always be free
  you Grays and Rights and Sperms
  you Blues and Humpbacks
Free to raise your calves
  swim blue waters with your mates

The truth is
When we have squandered all that you were
  blood and bone and breath
  we will be back
We will return for your brothers
We will return for all the others

# After…

we make love
you sleep on my bed.
The line of your back,
flare of hip,
length of thigh
remind me
of Picasso's *Blue Nude.*
I dare not breathe
lest you stir,
the moment lost
to memory.

# Red

there is the brilliant Red of geraniums
in the early morning light
the pale Red of an evening sky
when the sun turns the corner

there is the Red of wine and blood
spilled during love and battle
the Red of passion
in that battle of love

there was the Red of embarrassment
before the world embraced sin
the Red of fear and anguish
of flesh and bone burning in hell

there is the Red of a tomato ripe
on the vine then thick in a sauce
the delicious Red of fettuccini
drowning in marinara

there is the petal Red
that seduces the hummingbird
the pot metal Red of a toy fire truck
lost under a child's bed

there is the chalky Red of old bricks
that lie in piles where a tenement house stood
the Red stench of the slaughterhouse
that lies in puddles on the floor

there is the Red of lips kissed
before the secrets they whisper
the Red of hearts broken
lovers scattered in the past

## La Jolla Shores

we venture beyond trivial waters
to the distant rising of the sea
where giants march toward shore
and lift us to the sky

## Finding a Poem...

      at the beach is more difficult
than I first imagined. With the cliché
of sea & sky so overwhelming, so strong
in its song of surf against shore, I fear
nothing will move me, my muse buried
beneath the collapse of a weekend sandcastle.
Then, within that smooth slope of sand,
pointed protrusions & right angles,
textures & lines not native to this place
in time. There, buried by the toss of tides
on supple earth a rough hewn timber
draws me near. Labor & my curiosity
reveal its full length & breadth, the notch
at one end, holes for fitting—what?
Its geometry like a bench along the shore.
I sit & question this mute intruder,
the wind & sea—then myself. What
do I know of those great oak & fir
that die under the saw to birth timbers
like the one beneath me? What do I know
of this derelict wedge of a tree, its journey
in the sea?—Nothing.
But I do know, finding a poem at the beach
is more difficult than I first imagined.
Blinded by the cliché of sea & sky
you might miss the obvious,
                without a poet's eye.

# Kings Canyon
Summer of '57

Giant sequoias pierce the sky,
cradle clouds, shoulder the sun.

Under this ancient canopy
silent shadows dapple the earth.

A breeze carries campfire smoke,
laughter of children in the woods.

Rain drops spawn a soft patter
on forest floor, announce a storm.

Wild carnations, pledged to meadow
grass, bow shyly as wet swans.

Snow lingers in shaded shallows
beneath bold outcroppings of shale.

I hike among towering redwoods,
each an unfamiliar landmark.

In a small stream posted *No Fishing*
I catch my first cutthroat.

# Tide Pool

An Egret stands statue-like
atop a small spire of beach rock,
white plumage stark against a denim sky.
In a shallow hollow of sand a sea star
lies stranded by the retreating ocean.
It will be hours before the tide turns.
This is nature's way. There is no blame
to be placed. Yet, you feel obligated
to return this creature to deeper waters.
Nearby, half a mussel shell, remnants
of seagulls foraging. The shell is slender,
slightly scooped, perfect for your needs.
You slip it under the creature's belly,
carry her to the deepest edge of the tide pool.
As she sinks slowly to the bottom
one of her arms moves ever so slightly.
A "Thank You" wave?

## Vestido Rojo

On a beach in Manzanillo
fishing boats lie overturned, lined up
like contestants in a beauty contest.
Pulled high on the sand to avoid tides
they soak up a fresh coat of paint.
Many, that blue hue of a cloudless
summer sky. Others, green as chili
verde served at Carmen's Cantina.

I find a place in the shade, watch
fishermen repair their nets, share
stories of the sea. There is a poem
somewhere among these faces,
weather worn hands, sheen of wet paint.

Beyond the boats a woman walks
at water's edge, shoes in hand.
A red dress hugs her ample hips,
reveals cleavage of such proportions
a careless lover might be lost forever
in its depths. I came to write about
these men and their boats. Yet,
just as the bull cannot control
his charge at the matador's cape,
I leave the fishermen to their chores,
chase after that woman in the red dress.

## This Morning...

    I thought of you:
the warmth of your body against mine;
that fragrance of your hair when I kissed your neck;
the taste of your mouth;
your sighs of pleasure;
that boundless blue of your eyes.

This morning I thought of you and fell in love
again.

# Mount St. Helens
May 18, 1980

Today the sea whispers her secrets
to me, though she has not always
been my neighbor. In those years
that survived our youth, we roamed
the conifered coast of Oregon;
climbed mountains that bled rivers
into the Pacific; stalked salmon
and steelhead; watched a generation
of alder and Douglas fir fall amidst
a cacophony of chain saws; waited
hours for a shot at elk that foraged
in coastal scrub dense as
                    a Robert Lowell poem.
And always the cloud cluttered sky,
formations that looked like banks
of rock, watched over us.
Then, that day in May stone
and sky were one with a torrent
of molten rock as uprooted
forests flowed down cindered slopes.
And ash rose into the stratosphere,
an impersonal gray coat draped
across the shoulders of the earth.
All we could do was watch
from that small meadow where
we stopped to pick huckleberries.
I can still recall the way trees quivered,
Jays fell silent and how tightly
you held my hand.

# Proposition

Come with me to Paris,
where food is a religion,
love affairs short lived
as clean sheets in a bordello.
I'll buy you the Eiffel Tower
or maybe your own bridge
on the River Seine. We'll stroll
the boulevard, watch artists
struggle with color and light.

But here, in this California
beach town, all I can offer
are craggy coastal bluffs,
a stretch of sand stippled
with impressions of lovers
and the blood of a setting
sun spilled across the sea.
The only Parisian pleasure
I can promise is a French kiss.

# Revisiting

I recognize this place
where one summer night

I scattered the ashes
of my last love affair

with a girl whose name
now keeps me up nights.

I saw shooting stars
in her eyes as pale moonlight

played across her thighs.
And her kiss, yes—her kiss.

# The Arts

I have finished the painting:
profuse amounts of pigment sculpted
across a canvas with a palette knife,
the way a mason grouts a brick façade.
Painting, like poetry, is the reckless
replacement of what you already have,
the hope something with energy emerges.
I'm never sure if I am finished.
(the paintings, the poems)
So, when I lay down the knife and the poem
will accept no further revision,
I have no place to go, no reason to remain.

## Morning Rain

Most days mourning doves wake me
with their love songs. The occasional
bus, belly filled with commuters, rattles
and hisses somewhere beyond the trees.
A leaf blower whines in the distance.
But today, the ping of raindrops on the pane
tells me there will be no morning serenade,
and the gardener, if he is smart, is sipping
coffee somewhere under cover. Wind whips
a tree branch against the house, a wild animal
on the attack. My bedroom window emits
a whistle that mimics the storm, like Sachmo's
trumpet surrendering to his billowed cheeks.
I pull the covers over my head, slip into sleep.
Outside, rain falls in sheets that hang
from heaven to earth, like God's laundry on a line.

## We Were There

We were there in The Haight, flowers in our hair,
beads around our neck; doe eyed girls bared their breasts,
brandished bras; boys, not yet men, burned draft cards,
numbers in the devil's lottery, political punishment
                                    for being born.
We were there when napalm obliterated human decency,
burned babies in their mother's arms, denied innocence
                            to those still in the womb.
We were there to see the oxidized eyes of dead come home
in boxes draped in broken promises; to hear dirges sung
like lullabies, lyrics that languished, lost graveside,
names resurrected decades later, etched on the headstone
                                    of history.
We were there, but turned away from that pile of bones,
left our failures to rot in rice paddies,
                    in undefeated jungles.
We were there that Friday in Dallas, heard the shots,
saw everything, saw nothing, watched a nation's dreams
                    explode, puddle on the hot pavement.
We were there when chants rose like prayers
into the Memphis air, black and white brothers at last,
brothers at last, then the angry retort of smoke and lead.
                                    Martin dead.
We were there at Kent State. Protest. Nixon. Cambodia.
Open fire. Fight back with your books.

We were there. We survived.
        Today, we think the same thoughts of the soul.

# Blue

It's true, your eyes
are not the blue
of those morning glories
that drape
the downtown
library walls.

They are the blue
of an Arctic sky:
cool, crisp, cloudless,
with a blush of sunshine
that lights my world.

## Storm

There is that moment
when wind first finds the sea,
sweeps down & licks
at her liquid curves;
that moment when
the birth of a storm
is still in doubt,
whitecaps unimagined,
that turbulent mix
of cobalt & turquoise
only a possibility. But,
if the sea surrenders
to these overtures,
which she almost always
does, there is a tempest
no man can tame,
but only hope to survive
as cannon shots of thunder
& lightning strikes
make you wonder
if Ben Franklin
is somewhere in the clouds
flying his kite.

# Lily Pond

The sky has fallen
among the lily pads
in Monet's pond.

His Japanese bridge,
red as a storybook barn,
a crimson arc in the clouds.

In these still waters,
your reflection.
Not even Monet's brush
could capture such beauty.

# Erased

There was a woman
(But then, isn't there always?)

hair the color of caramel; curve
of her neck, all Audrey Hepburn;
a mouth that said everything
without whispering a single word.

I lost count of our time together:
days in a garden where roses
the shade of evening's failing sun
bloomed with reckless abandon;

nights in a room fresh from
a Van Gogh painting, our bodies
blanketed by starlight that fell
through naked window panes.

She left one day. Not even a good-bye.
I've erased the entire affair from my mind.

Did I mention her hazel green eyes,
how they always caught me by surprise?

# The Last Reading
### —for George

*...I live in the moment,* was the last line
of the last poem read by a poet I barely knew,
the last words I heard him speak. Maybe
the last words he spoke to anyone.

He does not speak to me mere minutes later
as I kneel over him in the parking lot,
his arms tight against his body, fists clenched,
face flushed, the faint throb of a pulse in his neck,
—or is there?

I cradle his head in my hands and tell him,
*Help is on the way.* He does not speak
and I sense he has crossed into eternity. Still,
I try to force life into the mouth of death
while a stranger pumps that frail chest,
attempts to do what a failed heart cannot.

A dozen police arrive, then, paramedics
who work on him nearly half an hour.
Every time they stop CPR the monitor flat-lines.
So they gather up their equipment and leave
a blue plastic bundle lying on the pavement
waiting for the Coroner.

# Beyond Tidewater...

a meld of kayaks and ocean.
The slow tolling of a buoy bell
announces the cadence of a rising sea.

On the distant shore, immorality
prejudice and greed lie in wait.
Weeds among the wildflowers.

So we linger, enraptured by the bark
of a sea lion, swooping flight of pelicans
and friendship's silence.

# Birthing

I went to a reading,
a celebration,
a publication party
for local poets.
No one else came.

An old man
selling copies
of the Anthology
sat in the corner.
I bought them all.
Rent would have to wait
—again.

I read to that vacant room,
first page to last.
Not one clap unfolded
from those empty chairs.

But, I did
what had to be done:
I mid-wifed words,
gave them life.

Because a poem
written on the page
but unspoken,
is an unborn child.

# Beach Bum's Lament

The sun has just begun to show
though it is nearly noon.

I watch waves break on shore,
listen to their death rattle,

that final explosion of power
that erodes the very edges of Earth.

Gulls lurk nearby, hoping for a share
of my sandwich. Scattered along the sand,

groups of beachgoers, folding chairs
with built-in umbrellas, beach blankets

held down by huge coolers. A breeze
out of the west whispers life's secrets.

But, I don't speak the language
so catch only a word or two.

## Surf Safari

In the cab of my truck, coffee cup cradled
between my hands, steam streaks the windshield.
Outside, the Pacific pounds against a beach I knew
in my childhood. I have returned, not through
some portal in the space time continuum,
not beamed here by a Star Trekish transporter,
rather by a simple drive up Coast Highway.

I unload my board and make that long walk
across sand already hot from the morning sun,
across sand I have crossed a hundred times,
across sand marked with the footprints of my youth.

I step into the sea and paddle into the past,
out through waves of memory, where
fear was an unknown word, where we knew
there would always be another tomorrow.

In this cold water I wait for swells
to build, sun warm on my bare shoulders,
on my skinny sixteen-year-old frame. Friends
nearby laugh and talk that nonsense of youth.

Finally, frigid waters take their toll. We head
for the beach to huddle in the sun, lie about
those great waves we caught, whistle at girls,
throw sand and be young.

I feel a tug on my shoulder, turn to look
into the face of an old man—my surf buddy.
*Wake up,* he insists. *We can still catch
the senior special breakfast at Denny's.*

## Bus Bench

This bench, where the raucous rattle
of Harleys cruising 101 slams
into my ears like a sledgehammer,
where grit stirred up by passing cars
finds its way into my hair, where
the Pacific fans out below the bluff;
this bench, scarred with carved images
by graffiti artists, worn from decades
of commuters waiting on their workday;
this bench is the only place I'm sure
of seeing you on your afternoon walk.

## Sedona

Red rock pinnacles hold up the sky.
Saguaros stand silent: lonely sentinels
along desolate desert highways.
Rain clouds sling shadows
across Castle Rock while to the east
Bell Rock glows in early light.
At Montezuma Well spirits
of the Sinagua Indians speak a language
long forgotten, found only
in the precise memory of carved rock.

## I Wander the Beach...

in search of
unbroken seashells.

They are as rare
as unbroken hearts.

I spot one half buried
in the sand.

Closer inspection
reveals an imperfection.

The shell was to be a gift,
a symbol of my love.

Now, this poem will have to do.
This, and every kiss I give you.

# Black's

Out of the northeast
a murmur of summer wind
this December day.

The sea, silent beneath
towering cliffs of opulence,
awakens,

rises from the depths
as beguiling emerald walls
pleading for our touch.

# Letter to General Paul Tibbets, (1915-2007)
—pilot of the Enola Gay

> *War is hell.*
> General William T. Sherman,
> Union Army


General Tibbets, I was saddened by the news of your death.
Yet, 92 years is more than most of us can hope for
and I suspect more than you ever imagined
as you flew that deadly mission back in '45.

It seems like a lifetime ago, those thousands of souls
exchanged for an un-know number of U.S. service men saved.
My father fought in that war and survived
to return home and raise a family—
maybe because of what you did that August day.

I could have been a child, like thousands of others,
who knew his father only from pictures on the mantle
or visits to the cemetery. A child denied
a father's strong hands of guidance and praise.

It's difficult to embrace the fact my life was blessed
by a Phoenix like fortress named after your mother;
by the un-Godly force released from a five ton
cylinder dubbed *Little Boy*; by the death of 100,000 souls.

But General, what I find so frightening
is that we have learned so little—after burying so many.

# Buffalo

I am Buffalo.
In the days after the first moon
I was thunder across the prairies,
a pageant of dust that settled on the sun.
I was as many as the blades of grass,
the earth trembled beneath my hooves.
Long before this land had a name
the Indian came and we were brothers.
He took what he needed, nothing more.

I am Buffalo.
My brother danced and sang my name
in his lodge, painted his face for the hunt.
I gave myself, my flesh for food, my hide
for warmth, my bones for tools.
Glorious death, then I lived forever in legend.
Buffalo. I was revered

—until the Anglo.
You came with horses and guns,
your ignorance and greed.
I ran from your bullets but you killed me
again and again,
ripped the hide from my carcass,
left my flesh to rot in the sun;
prairie red with blood,
the stench of slaughter.

You killed me to starve the Indian.
You killed me for sport
from your iron horse.
You killed me and laughed,
to impress a woman,
to win a bet, to pass the time.
You murdered me,
and never gave it a thought.

I am Buffalo.
Never again will the thunder be heard,
the earth tremble, the sun fade
in the sod churned by multitudes.
Now you struggle to rescue me
from your own hand.

I am Buffalo.
Back from the grave,
from the mountains of bleached bones,
back from the slaughter.

      Not because I am revered.
      Not because we are brothers.
      But, because you are ashamed.

## Secrets of a Rose

On my morning walk
I stop at a neighbor's garden,
admire a late blooming rose.
Her petals are the color
of morning's failing moon;
that long line of her stem,
emerald as the hills of Ireland;
and those thorns, lethal I'm sure.
I know to handle her with care.
After days in a crystal vase
her fragrance fills my every
breath; her beauty still catches
me by surprise. But, there is still
one unanswered question. So,
I pluck her petals one by one:
*she loves,*
*she loves me not,*
*she loves me.*

*Yes—she loves me.*

# Father's Tackle Box

It sits in the corner of the garage
cloaked in that gray dust of neglect,
two shades of green with silver clasps,
compartments for hooks and jigs,

lures and line, weights and bobbers.
The hours it spent, lid thrust open
like the gaping maw of a drowning fish,
waiting for my father's hand to pull

the secrets from its depths, sort them out
from the rusted hooks and broken lures,
to cast them into the sea and wait
under that warm Mexican sun.

Now, the lid closed tight, that time
of warm waters and bright days hidden
away, only to be revisited when my father
once again sees my mother's smile.

# Daisies

I watch the daisies
nestled in their clay pot
quiver in the breeze.

They stare back,
yellow faces, white manes:
a pride of lions
lazing in the afternoon sun.

## Storm

Unlike Sandburg's fog
that *comes on little cat feet,*

this storm slashes the air,
drums a syncopated rain

on my window pane,
while wind rattles the bones

of this young January,
tosses trees to their knees.

And that chill—
that deep chill that finds you

even under Grandma's quilt.

# French Lavender

An ocean breeze
walks its way
down our street.
Wind chimes
on the neighbor's porch
become restless.
That delicate clink
of glass shards
fractures the silence.
I open a window,
let in the breeze.
With it, the fragrance
of lavender
grown from seeds
you smuggled back
from France. I recall
the customs inspector,
that smile you flashed,
and your claim of:
*Nothing to declare.*
Even I believed that smile.

## With You
—for Katie Rose

Imagine roses shunned
by bees and hummingbirds;
the lily pond without Monet;
a September sunset absent
that blood red sky.

Imagine an opera unsung;
a poem unspoken;
a thunder storm quiet as a prayer.

Imagine Autumn leaves,
colorblind, unwilling to let go;
the sun not sharing shadows;
a song lacking lyrics.

Now imagine everything
in its proper place
the way God intended.

Like the once shunned roses,
the heretofore unspoken poem
and unsung opera,

I am so much more with you
than I could ever be on my own.

# His Song

My father and I
sit in the sun.
He sleeps
in his chair.
I watch leaves
quiver
in an easy
afternoon breeze.
Across the road,
among tombstones,
beyond
a long line of cars
parked on a gravel path,
people gather
to say goodbye.
A lone trumpet
cries its rendition
of *The Old Rugged Cross*.
My father stirs,
cradled in sunlight,
and I wonder
how long
before I must select
his song.

# The Passing of Spring

The Doctor's manner
much too casual,
all considered.
He spit the word
into the air
where it spread
across the room,
malignant
in the very speaking.
And we,
unable
to breathe in acceptance,
choked
on those syllables,
knowing
they would divide,
grow,
unstoppable.
So we returned home
to cry,
to talk,
to be together,
mother and son,
her final spring.
Now,
that season distant,
images and memories
once thought
unforgettable
slip silent
into inaccessible
corners of the heart.
And today, I realize
I cannot recall
the color of my mother's eyes.

# Boy at the Beach

He picks up a stone,
its flat face as smooth

as his own, and takes aim
at a flock of resting gulls.

Their instant flight
a tight circle
in the December air.

They settle back in,
danger past.

Down the beach, the boy
searches for another stone.

# The Color of Blood

The morning paper lies
on the table, still sequestered
by a red rubber band,
soggy as poorly prepared French toast.
Nobody expected rain last night.
A story on page seven reads so matter-of-fact,
succinct as a headstone:

> *San Diego photographer*
> *mauled, eaten by a grizzly.*

I can't help but wonder who he left behind.
In his last minutes, before being gutted
like a fresh caught salmon, did he call out
their names, or turn to his God?

And what of the bear:
600 pounds of muscle and rage,
teeth the size of steak knives,
straight razors for claws.

It must have been her cubs foraging
in the berries. We will do anything
to protect our children. She couldn't
know he only wanted pictures:
she the star, he the paparazzi.

When park officials shot and killed her,
some thought it an injustice.
Others saw it only as
the color of blood on the snow.

# Highway 101

You are the highway: concrete and asphalt ribbons laced together, Puget Sound to Olympia, across the Columbia to Astoria, still fresh with the footprints of Lewis and Clark; down the conifered coast of Oregon, Tillamook, Siletz and Brookings; winding your way among the Redwoods, the vineyards of Mendocino and Sonoma; across the Russian River, Santa Rosa to Petaluma, Frisco to Malibu, San Juan Capistrano to Oceanside, down to the surf of San Diego. You are the highway of my youth, the highway of my memories, you are PCH, El Camino Real, the Roosevelt, the Olympic; you are highway 101.

Your curves carried me to the sea in that old Chevy, black fenders, chrome bumpers shimmering in the summer sun, windows down, wind cool against my face. You were the highway, whispering promises I remember to this day. I followed your double yellow past sprawling mansions in Long Beach, cracker-box homes in Seal Beach, down Main Street with her small shops and bars, the liquor store near the pier. You skirted the shambles of Surfside, that despair of cardboard hovels along Tin Can Beach, on to the opulence of Laguna, past the towering face of Dana Point, down to those calm waters of San Clemente.

You are the highway, the highway of my dreams, my highway of motorcycles and cars where I learned to love speed. You are the highway where I kissed the girls, discovered life and death before my time, leaned that old Harley into tomorrow; highway of foggy lanes and darkness, bridges and concrete abutments unforgiving as alcohol and blind corners. You are the highway that killed Brian, crushed his hopes inside a rusty V-Dub bus.

You are the highway of my sorrows, the highway I followed to
school, the highway that called me to surf when I should have
been in class. You were my undoing, led me astray some say,
made it easy to leave, you, the highway of my youth, a fool's
highway of dreams I traveled too often. You are the highway
I should blame, but even then I knew life was more than a Chevy
with glass-packs and baby moons, more than burgers and fries,
a midnight ride with my buddies, more than a bottle of wine, girls
who didn't care where we parked. You were the highway, the one
I chose to follow, feel the speed, that need to be someplace else.
You are the highway—my highway, and I don't regret
a single day in that fast lane of our past.

# In Search of the Esquire Girl

They smiled back at me
from between thick glossy pages,
seduction in their eyes,
a suggestive suggestion on pouty lips.

At least, that's the way I saw it,
a boy of 12, sneaking a peek,
savoring every image
of those Esquire girls of the fifties:
Brigitte, Marilyn, Jane.

Now, when my Esquire magazine
arrives I wonder what
has gone wrong with the world.

This month, George Clooney adorns
the cover, a campy black and white photo.
Where is the Esquire girl? Where
is her smile, that implied seduction?

And when I open the magazine,
it's as if I've wandered
into some back street bordello.
But it's only a *peel and sniff* page
for an overpriced men's cologne.

Then, an ad for Ralph Lauren:
a male model glares at me,
hair perfect, penetrating eyes,
straight nose and strong chin.
My God, he's magnificent.
But where is the Esquire girl?

Next, a double spread for Prada:
again, four young men, boys really,
very pretty boys. Not a zit
or a cowlick in the bunch—nor a smile.

And then a piece for Armani:
two men, angular faces, brooding
eyes, one with a two day stubble
and rectangular designer eyeglasses.
I can almost understand why some men
choose to switch sides.
But where is the Esquire girl?

More pages of Gucci, Land Rover,
Calvin Klein and Tommy Bahama,
all touted by beautiful men who can't
seem to find all their shirt buttons.

Then finally, back on page 116,
a blond in six inch heels and lace panties,
her legs longer than a Mark Twain sentence.
Seated on the edge of a bed she gazes
over her shoulder, right into my eyes.
She's all Esquire girl.

But why back here, following
a hundred pages of pretty, pouting men?
Has there been a hostile take-over
by Redbook or Woman's Day?

Alas, Esquire, not what it once was.
But then, who among us is?

# I Went to Tucson for a Week

I journeyed across desolate desert sands
singing with the blush of spring. Giant saguaro,
arms raised in praise, offered blossoms to the sun.
The song of tires on hot asphalt, speeds that tease
radar, I flew by Painted Rock Road, Casa Grande
and past Picacho Peak. El Centro, Winterhaven, Yuma
in the morning behind me; Tucson, sprawling, spilling
south out of the Lagunas in the blue distance.

I went to Tucson for a week
   to eat beans for lunch with my dad,
   to spread new gravel in his driveway,
   to see old Buicks rusting in back yards,
   to feed the finches and doves,
   to hear mariachi music explode
      from low rider Chevys.

I went to Tucson for a week
   to watch rabbits hop along the back fence,
   to be annoyed by the F14s out of Davis,
   to trim a mulberry tree.

I went to Tucson for a week
   to have coffee with Snow Birds,
   to dodge old pickups driven by even older Hispanic men,
   to be amazed at how many kids you can raise
      working for minimum wage,
   to eat ice cream before dinner—then again after,
   to see mourning doves in pairs, perched
      on a wire fence.

I went to Tucson for a week
   to listen to dogs bark sunrise to midnight,
   to buy tortillas and carne asada
      at the corner tienda,
   to watch my father ride his bike three times
      around the park—not bad for 85.

I went to Tucson for a week
   to wander through neighborhoods in search
      of a blade of grass,
   to watch Lawrence Welk reruns,
   to hear sentences that begin in the middle,
   to scatter bird seed under the mulberry
      watch quail scratch
      and dance in the gravel,
   to listen to stories told again and again—and again.

I went to Tucson for a week
   to watch a cactus wren gather twigs for her nest,
   to wait in the shade of the porch for something
      to happen—anything.

I went to Tucson for a week to feel the hot wind
   on my face and wish for the sound of surf
      —that never comes.

# The Price of Renovating Downtown

Ancient adobe buildings squat
in the shadows of steel and glass towers
in old downtown Tucson.

Doorways huddle against the sidewalk,
stare into that cobbled street. Wooden gates
that guard small yards sag on rusted hinges.
Weeds thrive in sidewalk cracks.

In stunning contrast, every door on the street
is painted a brilliant blue or red or green.

An old man stands in a doorway,
his face as weathered as the buildings.
His side of the street now in the cold
shade of downtown renovation.

I approach to inquire about the doors.
He turns his back, slips into the dim light.
Someday soon he will be forced
to find another street of painted doors.

# Imagining Flowers

Imagine if you can, God
in the midst of creation.
On the third day it's time
for the first flowers to bloom.
But God does not carpet Earth
with pastel petals, thorns
and unimaginable fragrances.

Instead, He turns the task over
to an angel of lesser talent
who decides to place a *post-it*,
bearing only the word *flower*
on each plant, hoping
God will fill in the details later.

Imagine the Hummingbird's frustration
as she flits from one non-description
of a honeysuckle to the next.
Imagine your lady's dismay
when you hand her a bouquet of *post-its*,
promising that subtle scent of roses
when God gets around to the specifics.

Imagine now, if you can, you are a poet
and believe your every word a flower:
long stems placed in a crystal vase;
petals scattered at the feet of royalty;
essences extracted, their seductive
scents adorning beautiful women.

Ah yes, the words of angels and poets
passed off as flowers. And God just smiles
at our attempts to imitate His work.

# Afternoon at the Pool

On the deck old men with skinny
legs talk about the price of gas
& the best place in town to get
a good steak. The pool water
resonates with casual conversations
of women in sun hats. The hot tub
simmers like a witch's caldron.
I lay my book down, the latest
Grisham tale, and lie back
in the chaise. A train rumbles
in the distance. Overhead, gulls
squawk & circle their nest where
new hatchlings cry for food.
Like a child I search the sky
& its afternoon collection of clouds
for familiar shapes. There should be
elephants & butterflies & a tiger or two,
                    yet, I see only you.

# Believer

In this lazy beach town,
just north of that chaotic
Mexican border,
there is a set of stairs
down to the sea.

On the fragile face
of this bluff a drape
of passionate purple
blooms: a native plant
whose name escapes me,
if I ever did know it.

On a good day
storm swells march in,
collide with a shallow reef
just off shore, shoot skyward.
A perfect wave some say.

I sit silently in my truck,
sip hot coffee and wait.
I have faith in the forecast
of a coming south swell,
just as mankind clings
to the hope of heaven.

# Letter From God

Yesterday I received a letter from God, not one of those mental
images that rattles around in your head, a single pea in a pod, nor
did it cause me to speak in tongues or burst into flames, it was an
*honest-to-God* letter printed on scenic stationary, the Sea of
Galilee I believe, yet, there was no return address, though the
*forever* stamp was cancelled in San Diego, a fact the Chamber of
Commerce could capitalize on, *San Diego, home of the Chargers
& God,* but the idea that God uses the US Postal Service to
spread His message scares the hell out of me, so I saved the
letter, slipped it into my Bible, & while we're on the subject I just
can't get into Bible stories, take Adam & Eve, he sends her to the
marketplace for fruit, specifically asks for pears but Eve brings
back an apple, tells Adam the produce guy sssssaid one bite could
change their lives, get them out of that rut they're in, eat, sleep,
eat, sleep, lie around naked, & we're supposed to believe all
mankind has since been cursed, burdened with daily chores,
weeds in the garden, a mortgage, a spouse that won't shut up,
& the certainty of death because Eve picked a round fruit instead
of one shaped like J.Lo, & then there's the Ark, centuries of
human unrest, debauchery & toga parties so God decides to wipe
us out, but save the animals, even the serpents, go figure, then
Noah & Sons come in with the low bid, begin construction right
there in the front yard, ignore the zoning laws & codes, & what a
great idea, put the lions & antelope together in a confined space
for forty days & forty nights, but today PETA would protect
those poor animals even as millions of humans go hungry &
homeless, & God promises everlasting life, that is, if the mail
carrier doesn't lose your letter.

# Sunday Shoes

I don't own a pair
of Sunday shoes,
leather tanned
from the hide
of an unborn calf,
supple
as a woman's thigh.

Shoes
stitched in Italy,
in small shops
on cobbled streets
where once
Caesar's legion marched,
where today
motor scooters scurry,
beautiful women
perched on the back
clinging
to their lovers.

Sunday shoes
are saved for church
and funerals
as if God, or the dead,
care
about footwear.

## The Morning After...

        I awake
with the fragrance
of your hair
still in the air.

Your last laugh
languishes
on my pillow.

Tangled sheets
speak to me
about your body.

I slip back into sleep,
hope to find you
in my dreams.

# Vindication

Under the eave a brilliant yellow dance
of wasps building a nest. I watch with wonder
that delicate papery cone take shape. Small
symmetrical chambers agape, waiting
                    for the seeds of new life.

But, my granddaughter is visiting today.
She will play in that yard, on this porch.
And I know the wasps do not understand
my love for her, how I would do anything
                        to keep her safe.

So, with nothing more than my suspicions,
without ever questioning their intent,
I take that old straw broom from the closet,
and with one mighty sweep—kill them all.

Man can justify anything,
in the name of love.

# Café Encounter

There's a momentary lull in that un-intelligible murmur of café
conversations. And, almost as if on cue, she enters wearing a
fedora like men wore in the fifties and a pair of Levi's that fit in
a way Mr. Strauss never imagined. A blond waterfall spills from
beneath her hat, frames perfect features, tumbles down her
shoulders. Silver rings adorn several fingers, an uncountable
number of ornate bracelets hug her left wrist, huge hoop earrings
dangle against her neck. He can't help but wonder if there are
other jewels attached in more intimate places. Almost as if
reading his thoughts she looks his way, a suggestion of a smile on
her lips. He notices the black leather belt encircling her waist, its
enormous silver buckle like those given as trophies to rodeo stars.
Immediately he conjures up images of this woman atop a Brahma
bull, dominating for the required eight seconds before turning the
animal loose to sulk in his pen. She catches him again, watching
her. He should know better, ignore her. This is what got him in
trouble last time. But he remembers the words of a wise poet who
wrote, *I learn by going where I have to go.* So, he peeks over his
morning paper, shifts into surveillance mode. Why isn't this
woman wearing a diamond on her ring finger? Is she the type
who slips off her vows before leaving home, to tease, make men
wonder, fantasize? Or is she cold and hard, refusing to give
herself to anyone? As he ponders this she approaches his table.
*237 Maple Street, apartment 7,* she says, then turns and walks
out. At this moment his woman returns to their table. *Your face is
flushed, are you all right?* she asks. *I'm fine,* he says. Then, in the
most casual tone he can muster at the moment, he inquires,
*Is there a Maple Street around here?*

## Discreet

Email is a private affair,
quiet and tidy
in its electronic envelope.
No chance
of someone finding
those words
from your lover
in an old coat pocket,
slipped between
the pages of a book
or in the bottom
of a drawer.
And someday,
when relatives
collect earthly items
left behind,
there will be
no bundle of indiscretion
tied neatly
with an old ribbon.

# Down to the Sea
For David Martin, killed by a great white April, 2008

David Martin is lifted from the sea
like a man pulled from the submersion
of baptism, soul offered up to God,
a sacred sacrament of surrender.

Why is David the chosen one?
Is it the shape his body makes in the ocean,
a silhouette so similar to a sea lion,
maybe mistaken for a sick struggling seal?

Questions that remain unanswered
as the Great White rushes toward the surface,
ghost like lids closed over cold black eyes,
jaws agape, row upon row of serrated teeth exposed.

David Martin cries out the name of his God
as he is heaved from ocean waters
into the chilly morning air, his blood
staining the sea, before being dragged below,
the Pacific drowning his screams.

There will be no triathlon, no celebration
of his personal victory, no finisher's tee-shirt,
no trophy, no photos, no plans for the next event.

The waters off Solana Beach roil
with the thrashing of arms and legs,
caudal and dorsal fin—then silence.
The Great White has realized her mistake.
Yet, there are no apologies as she swims
out to sea still in search of her next meal.

A flotilla of primordial instincts dwells
just off shore, and those of us
who go down to the sea—pray for God's mercy.

118

## Ol' Paint

I can recall the day I got that ol' paint, down
around San Anton. Five-card stud was the game
if I recollect. Some young drover come up short
when I tossed a twenty dollar gold piece in the pot.
But that cowboy just wouldn't let it slide.
He leaned back in that bar room chair an' said,
with a confident air, *I'll call with that fine animal
tied outside.* He made his small straight,
but I filled my flush an' asked him
to kindly remove his saddle from my horse.

It's been a decade an' maybe a couple seasons more
since I first tied my bed roll atop that ol' gal.
We chased cattle an' choked down dust
from the Texas Panhandle all the way to Santa Fe
that paint an' me. We worked wild horses
out near Pueblo the spring of '82, then spent
the better part of five years just driftin' an' growin'
old together, the way a cowboy an' his horse do.

Now, I wish I'd never turned over that last card
all those years ago, but how was I to know.
This mornin' that ol' paint just looked up at me
with them big black eyes, like she knew.
There's only so much a cowboy can do
for his horse, an' I did the only thing I could.
The last thing I'll ever do for that ol' gal.

# Poet's Perception

I sink into the gray of this first day
of winter, a morning sky streaked
with pale fingers of sunlight.

In this muted chaos pelicans glide
into sight, a great winged string
of beads dropped by an angel.

I watch as they stream above me,
swoop down, skim the sea. Now,
the moment lost—except in memory.

But when the time comes to revisit
this hour with words, the poet's pen
may remember the skies as a woman's

blue eyes and soft smile, while
the string of pelicans will no doubt
become pearls draped about her.

# Visiting Hours

I spend the morning
with my father
in the V.A. hospital.
He lies silent beneath
sheet and blanket
perfectly smoothed
with their crisp
military corners.

An old woman
cleans the sink,
his bedside table.
She pays no attention
to the tubes and wires,
digital readouts,
that low hum
of nearby machines.

I can think of nothing else.

# My Father and I Make Bricks in the Backyard

When I was a boy, there was a time when my father
returned home from his day as a milkman,
went out to the backyard and made bricks:
red concrete bricks cast in forms fashioned from
2 X 4s and plywood, each exact in its dimensions.
My father forged bricks in this manner for months
—six bricks a day.

The wheelbarrow, the cement, the sand,
the aggregate, the water, the measuring,
the mixing, the form, the brick.

He let them set up overnight before sliding each
from its wooden cocoon and laying it along
the fence to cure. Only then did he mix more concrete
in that rusty wheelbarrow he kept behind the garage.

It was my job to spray those new bricks with water
every day. *Slow curing makes strong bricks,*
my father would say. And then he would show me again
how to bathe them in a fine mist from that old
garden hose we kept coiled beneath the avocado tree.

The hose, the spray, the curing, the brick.

Then one day he said, *We have enough bricks son,
let me show you how to mix mortar.*
His trowel flashed in the sunlight like a saber
as he mixed the mud and told me how bricks
are of little value without mortar.

The wheelbarrow, the cement, the sand,
the water, the measuring, the mixing,
the trowel, the mortar, the brick.

122

My father built planters with our bricks:
their crimson contour clinging to the patio wall,
encircling that old acacia in the parkway,
embracing our tidy stucco house.

Yesterday, I returned to my childhood home
half a century after my father and I
cast the first brick in our backyard.

Those planters still stand—straight and strong,
like my father all those years ago.

Those planters still stand—a monument
to the wheelbarrow, the measuring,
the mixing, the form, the trowel, the brick.
A monument to those days of father and son.

# Mistress

She never loved me the way I *wanted* her.
We met quite by chance, but then
that's the way of the universe, unplanned
moments that become the rest of your life.

She was reluctant in the beginning. So,
I made promises I could not keep, spent money
as if I had it and took her home with me.

We spent seasons together. Winter evenings
her warmth cradled in my hands. Spring,
she lay with me on the cool grass
of afternoon. But she never loved me.

Come summer, our relationship burned
like a stretch of sand beyond tide's reach.
She taught me the language of the sea,
how to ask the sun for a crimson night sky.

Then, fall brought a brooding moon
and she held her words inside. Even
though she invited me in, to search
them out, taste their secrets, feel her
on my tongue, she never loved me.

So it was, year upon year, I gathered her in,
pressed the rest of the world from between us,
listened for the essence of her sighs
and realized she may never love me.

Then, on a day when I believe I can
no longer call myself *Poet*, she comes
to me, like the moon finds the night,
slow and easy. My muse surrenders,
gives herself completely
and I take her for my mistress.

# The Bench

Alongside his house a bench:
varnished wood, rough cast iron
facing the morning sun.

Not long ago he could see
the ocean from this bench.
Then, men came in trucks
loaded with lumber and saws,
the occasional dog.

He watched the sea disappear
behind a gray veneer
of sheetrock and siding:
a fog that will never lift.

The neighbor's new house
throws down a shadow
that creeps toward his feet
like some mutant creature
out of a 50's horror movie.

And that sea breeze,
which once played among
the Mandevilla, must now fight
its way past porch railings
and a white plastic fence
that stands guard around
his neighbor's unplanted lawn.

He rarely sits on the bench now,
its varnish curled, cast iron rusty.
Instead, he clings to fading images
of sea and sky, the way you might
conjure up the face of an old lover.

# Confessions of an Ensenada Cruise

I was here a year ago,
walked these dirty streets
with their trinket stands
and hucksters chanting
practiced English spiels
thick with the voice
of their heritage.

And the children are still here:
those street corner beggars,
faces smudged with poverty;
hands extended for the coins
of Gringo pity, or embarrassment.

I give a woman a dollar,
ask if I may take a picture
of her three-year-old daughter
selling bracelets on the sidewalk.

Later, I drop two quarters
into the palm of a brown angel
hawking Chiclets along the highway.

Returning to the ship for dinner,
where people will leave more
on their plates than those children
will have to eat for the next week,
I cannot escape my decisions of today:

ten dollars
for a tee-shirt for my granddaughter,
who has everything;
a dollar and a half
for two children who have nothing.

## Sarah

It was spring, crocus in full bloom,
mornings crisp and clear. Afternoon
sun slipped through the window
and I basked in its warmth.
Somehow, I put her out of my mind.

Now, I awake a dozen times a night.
I feel her knees in my back, poke
of her elbow, smell her hand lotion,
feel the warmth of her body close by.

But when I turn to her—I'm alone.
Sometimes I get up,
sit on the porch in the dark,
whisper her name and watch to see
if a star twinkles at me.

# Saturday Auction

My ol' truck just couldn't make it
from town to the ranch,
so I pulled in at Charlie's Auction Yard
to let 'er cool down, like I did most every
Saturday afternoon. I cussed an' kicked
the running board, then wandered out back
where they keep the livestock.

First time I saw 'er, I knew she's somethin' special.
She weren't the prettiest, that ol' buckskin Mare,
standin' alone in the auctioneer's pit.
Jus' a wore-out ol' saddle bronc.

I could see right off, she'd been rode hard over the years,
them scars, up an' down 'er neck and shoulders,
from cowboy spurs, jabbin' an' slicin' for decades,
eight seconds at a time.

An' that look in 'er eyes, like she don't trust no one.
But she held 'er head high, kinda proud like,
an' the way she moved, muscled an' smooth,
I was pretty cert'n she was more than
jus' some ol' rodeo horse, that couldn't
make the next call to the chute.

They called 'er number, but she balked
when the cowboy tried to lead 'er in,
pullin' hard again' the reins and rearin' 'er head,
like she knew this was the end of the line.

The auctioneer began his song, the numbers
weren't big, an' there weren't many takers.
Just a fat man that runs a rodeo south o' the border.
An' the guy from the slaughterhouse,
smokin' a big cigar, makin' his bid without even lookin'.
Just eight hun'erd pounds of dog food to him.

The auctioneer sang out,
*I got one-seventy-five, do I hear one-eighty?*
The only sound —
that ol' Mare pawin' at the concrete floor.
*Goin' once!*
*Goin' twice!*

Then I heard the bid, *Three hun'erd dollars!*
I turned to see who the fool was, an' realized
it was me.
I didn't have but two hun'erd on me,
but they took my word an' a handshake for the rest.

She ain't had a buckin' strap or a cowboy on her back since.
I never did give her a name, jus' call her Ol' Gal,
figur' she don' mind.
To this day, I don' know why I bought that ol' saddle bronc.
Some things ya do—just 'cause it feels right.

## Total Recall

I went to a poetry reading last night.
Lola (*somebody*), a poet from Florida,
recited her poems from memory.

I was impressed, and at the same time
depressed. I can't remember my social
security number, never mind 20 lines

of verse. So I returned home, vowed
to write a poem, commit it to memory.
Unable to think of a thing, I decided

to steal some of her material.
Maybe that part about her son learning
to speak Mandarin in only two years.

No, that wouldn't work. My son is 35
and still has difficulty with his native
tongue. What about her granddaughter

writing poetry at 22 months? I have
a granddaughter. But, at 8 months
she hasn't written a word. So, I'm still

looking for something to commit
to memory. Maybe I should go back
to my social security number.

# The Words...

   are everywhere. They hide
beneath my pillow at night
whispering among themselves;
parade across my face,
wake me again and again.

Words gather in my coffee cup,
scream and dance.
(from the caffeine I presume)
They follow me
to the shower, to the beach.

Words rattle around in my mind.
I find them in my pockets,
in the sandwich I make for lunch,
in my sock drawer.

The words are everywhere
—until I put pen to paper.

## Neighborhood Boys
*—for Jimmy, Brian and Richard*

There were four of us: good Catholic boys.
Our mothers sent us to church each Sunday
to sit in polished oak pews, to kneel and stand,
repeat prayers on cue, like performing some ancient
pagan ritual. They sent us to church to confess
our sins, say penance and receive the holy host
of communion. But, because we were boys,
we played football on the church lawn instead.

There were four of us: good Catholic boys.
Then, Jimmy lost his soul to a devil named cocaine.
Sister Mary Anne said Jesus would save our souls
—if only we'd ask. Jimmy never did
as far as I know. We were just boys
and played football on the church lawn instead.

We never saw Jimmy again. Years later
I read his name in the paper: arrested
during a liquor store robbery, the clerk shot
and killed. Jimmy didn't pull the trigger.
Claimed he didn't know his friend had a gun.
The Judge didn't care. The law was clear.

There were four of us: good Catholic boys
who played football on the church lawn,
growing into men when one night Brian
drove his van into a concrete bridge on PCH.
The Highway Patrol said it shouldn't have happened,
traffic was light, the sky clear, the road dry.
Yet, Brian died that night, none of us sure why.

Over the years I stayed in touch with Richard.
He made it back from Vietnam, but brought
the demons with him. His wife left, took the kids,
went to live with her parents in Michigan.
It seems to me he deserved better.
It seems to me they all deserved better.

I was in the old neighborhood the other day,
stopped by the church. The lawn is gone, paved over
for more parking. Inside, a line of sinners waiting
near the confessional. A few of the forgiven
scattered among the pews, heads bowed in silent prayer.
I know no good can come from second-guessing life,
but I've always wondered what might have been
if we had—

No,
the truth is—there were four of us: good Catholic boys
who played football on the church lawn instead.

## First Time

This is not the first time
I've been with you.
But, it is the first time
we have been together.

And, unlike that first time
someone steps into the sea,
wades out just far enough
to make it safely back to shore,

I am *in over my head,* drowning
in the ecstasy of being with you.

# Flight

Sky stretches
lifeless
horizon to horizon.
Lines of Pelicans
that filled these skies
yesterday, now
lines on the poet's page.
Words in flight
journey
margin to margin,
destination
known only
to the poet.

# The Drop In

He comes through the front door
the way a mouse enters your house:
uninvited. A boy of maybe nine or ten.
He steals past the poet at the podium,
almost unnoticed, begins to forage
at the refreshment table concentrating
on vanilla wafers and grapes.
Between poems, during the applause,
he finds his way to an empty chair
in the front row, which leads me
to believe this is not his first time.
Fists filled with munchies he nods at
the chair, *Is this seat taken?* Bits
of vanilla wafer spew forth. He sits
and listens intently, applauds with gusto
—until his grapes and wafers run out.
Then, as the speaker finishes a poem,
the boys stands, acknowledges the poet
with a slight bow and slips out the door.
I watch him skip down the sidewalk.
No doubt there is another reading in town,
or possibly an art exhibit he wants to attend.

# The Formula

I always write poetry on a piece of paper
before going to the computer, that first
draft at least. Sometimes it's on a napkin
from McDonald's or the back of another
poem I've revised for the tenth time.

Emotions are supposed to flow through
your fingers, the pen, lie naked on the page.
Besides, I like that intimate feel of pen
slipping, swirling, leaving words behind.
But today, I've gone straight to the computer.

This click-clack of keys, like the indifference
of a prostitute, gives little satisfaction
to the process. And spell check has marked
my page with so much red, it's as if the editor
from hell lives in the keyboard.

So I hit delete and grab a steno pad lying nearby.
Half a dozen pens are scattered on the table.
One, pocked with teeth marks, catches my eye.
*Yes, this one. I wrote a good poem with this one.*
So it begins, the exact science of writing poetry.

# Tuesday

I hold her in my arms. Tears soak my shirt.
Like a river overflowing its banks she spills
the early years into my open heart.
*I want you to know*, she says. I drink in
every word, thirsty for this woman's love.
I pray she is not merely a mirage, shimmering
just out of reach. Later, dinner dishes linger
on the counter; on the stereo Johnny Cash
sings about love *hotter than a pepper sprout;*
and we declare our love. What else is there to say?

## Bedroom Walls

If bedroom walls could talk
they might whisper secrets
of when lights are low,
when you and I give our bodies,
our hearts, to each other.

If bedroom walls understood
they would know how you
rock my world, steal the very
breath from my mouth
with your kiss; how that fire
of your touch lights my universe.

## Las Mujeres

Senor Neruda,
    or may I call you Pablo?

I've read your poetry
and many questions come to mind.

I loved every line in
*VIENTE POEMAS de AMOR.*
Forgive me Pablo,
my Spanish is very poor.

But I really want to ask about the women:
the lovers, the wives, those nameless whores
on the back streets of Santiago.

Others might also inquire
of your friendship with Lorca,
question his influence on you, yours on him,
the way stars and planets pull at each other.

But Pablo, it's really the women
that draw me in, like an ocean
unable to escape the moon's magnetism.

Yet in truth we both know
you cannot separate women and poetry.
Are they not the same?

When you catch a glimpse of denim blue sky,
do you not think of a woman's eyes?
When you touch a woman's body,
do you not believe there is a God?

And when you are with that woman,
do the words not come easier?
Words of ribbons and hair,
silk sheets and near silent sighs.
Naked phrases offered in praise
and seduction.

And with this done, do we then know
who we are? Was it such a moment
when you wrote,

*...and it follows that I am, because of you.*

God, I wish I had written that line.
But people who do not chase words
will not understand: only with poetry
can you drink the sky from cupped hands,
taste the clouds sweet as a woman's lips.

Pardon me Pablo for presuming to tell you
about poetry. But I too put pen to paper,
offer it to the world, to be consumed
or thrown out with tomorrow's trash.

So Pablo, mi amigo,
            tell me about the women.

## Swami's

A remnant of late moon
lingers in the morning sky
even as the sun
    dances on the sea.
Around me, enfolding me,
    the very blood of the earth.

Sea grass bends
and stands straight again.
Dolphins slip past, silent,
    with no concern of me.

Out beyond the edge
where sea and sky fall away
    the stains of a brown haze.

Alas—this is not heaven.

# Healing Waters

I sit in the shade of a gnarled coastal pine
this summer look-alike November day.
A line of pelicans stitch clouds to sky
above these sea scarred bluffs of Del Mar.
The bite of rotting kelp, sweetness of sunscreen,
and ocean mist memories fill my afternoon.

Evening catches me at my desk, a trained rat
trapped in the maze, where I stumble upon
my divorce decree still not filed away after
seven years. I toss it aside, this now inoffensive
missive, the stench of consequence
washed away by the river of time.

# Pointed Words

Having used every subterfuge
to rid myself of marriage
I finally found truth as effective
as the surgeon's scalpel
to remove all that was malignant.
Merely stating grievances,
like union members on a picket line,
did not rescind decade old vows.

So I confessed, once again,
to that purchase of a Harley
with dollars set aside for new carpet.
And, just for good measure,
I threw in the name of a woman,
the address of a local motel
and a date recent enough
to be unforgivable.

Yet, in dreams I dread,
I still stumble upon her words,
sharp as a butcher's blade.
If only she had packed them
along with the china, each
wrapped in a page from our past.
Instead, nightly she sticks them
between my ribs
like a prison yard execution.

# Finale

The wedding ring is gone
along with that groove on his finger
where it nestled all those years.
It took decades to shape that flesh.
Yet now, you'd never know
it was ever there. He slipped that circle
of commitment into his pocket
the day he filed for divorce, then laid
it on the dresser in his new apartment
where it gathered dust for months.
His divorce final, he slid that gold band
off the dresser, let it fall into his hand.
It was not as heavy as he remembered.
He walked to where the sea surged
up a cobbled beach. And in that moonless
night caught a glint of starlight
off that ring as he tossed it into the Pacific.

## Lonely Wind

This breath
of a distant storm,
cool on my face,
twisting my hair,
presses against me
like an anxious lover.

# The Swimming Pool

The elderly are careful
with their steps,
like a child
learning to walk.

Knees protesting,
they creep across
cool concrete
toward their savior
the swimming pool.

There, a speck of youth
lies submerged
in that warm
chlorine baptismal.

They slide,
oh so carefully,
into the waiting water.

Their burden
of body weight lifted,
they float
like ducks on a pond,
glide
like Tinker Bell
or Peter Pan.

The grace of youth
returned
—for the moment.

# Papier-mâché Oscars

The true movie stars are gone you know.
Bogart, Cagney and Edward G: those
Saturday matinee heroes and villains.
And their gangster dialogue died with them:
*OK you mug, start singin' or I'll fill you full o' lead.*

John Wayne, all American tough guy
always walked in profile, pigeon-toed.

Those singing cowboys, Roy and Gene,
chased the outlaws, shootin' and ridin'
hard, never ran out of bullets, never
had to rest their horses, never lost their hats
during a fight or broke a string
on their guitar—now that's a movie star.

Clark Gable, ears nearly as big
as his drinking problem,
and he'd never turn down his collar.

The true movie stars are gone you know.
Those sultry sirens: Elizabeth,
Marylyn and Sophia. Not a bare breast
or buttock in a single scene, just silk stockings
and torpedo bras, but how we wanted them.

And let's not forget Tracy and Hepburn,
great on screen. Better in bed? Enough said.
And Paul Newman, rebellious, misunderstood.
*What we got here is a failure to communicate.*
And Robert Redford, able to ride a horse,
climb a mountain or fall down a flight of stairs
and never muss his hair.

The true movie stars are gone,
The golden days of the silver screen
rusting away in Hollywood studio vaults.

Oh, there's still folks out there playing
at acting, getting twenty or thirty
million to do a film. Most of the takes
they're naked with some silicone
princess or computer enhanced hunk.

They're not movie stars, not true movie stars.
They're products pushed by greedy agents,
slick Madison Ave print, sold to the public
like Jimmy Dean pork sausage or
plastic shoes from China.
There's only one true movie star left:
ladies and gentlemen, I give you
*The eighth wonder of the world:* KING KONG.

He is truly a BIG star. He's got more roar
than Al Pachino ever dreamed of, he's taller
than Dustin Hoffman, but then, who isn't?
He's built better than Schwarzenegger, got more
hair on his chest than Sean Connery.
Admittedly, he lacks depth,
a little reminiscent of Tom Cruise.

KING KONG, the last true movie star,
and, a perfect gentleman.
Not once during filming did he try
to peek under Fay Wray's dress.

# Flight School
### —for Gordon

We were just killing time
hangin' out in the back of that PBY
when the starboard engine went silent
—then the other. Suddenly
I yearned for the citrus groves,
that dry heat huddled
between the trees of my childhood,
those odd jobs handed out
by a farm boy's father.
Flight school seemed like a poor choice.
I slipped into my life jacket,
watched the sea rush up at us.
Then, a sputter, like the sound
that old tractor made
when Dad let me drive through the groves.
Both engines fired.
I smelled the orange blossoms.

# Phoenix Rising

after the 2004 wildfires
in San Bernardino County

San Bernardino, a city of rich
& poor plagued by disaster.
Ashes still warm from fires rage
sizzle in the slide of mud released
by nude hillsides—& some say,
by the wrath of God. Barren brick
fireplaces litter the landscape like
the toes of a giant corpse pointing
to heaven. Small shrines stand
in remembrance, objects retrieved
from a past life, displayed on card
tables, singed blankets in driveways
where rusted skeletons of Fords & Toyotas
guard nothing. A lone tree stands between
charred memories, green buds bursting
from branches. How can that be?
*For Sale* signs spring up like weeds
in the neighborhoods & promises
of new construction raise hopes
like a tent revival evangelist.
San Bernardino: a city in ruins.
Yet, already the seeds of tomorrow
sprout in the still warm ashes of yesterday.

## Acapulco Street Vendor

A child confronts me
on the sidewalk.
Without a word
she offers
a small blue bowl.
I smile,
shake my head no.
She persists.
Big brown eyes
make a plea
heard even above
the diesel clatter
of a passing bus.
Nearby
the mother watches,
waits with more
blue bowls.
One bowl sold,
tortillas for dinner;
two bowls sold,
maybe some rice.
I buy a bowl,
know
it is not nearly enough.

# Ode to October

October in Southern California is not about that first
dusting of snow; the scramble to find tire chains and bags
of rock salt somewhere in the basement; that frustration
of a snow shovel with a broken handle; the frightening
realization that you forgot to order heating fuel for November.

October in Southern California is a swell sweeping down
out of the north, the slam of surf on shore, waves that give
themselves to the earth, unashamed lovers; long lines of pelicans
skimming wave tops; morning fog that drives fair weather beach
goers back to their cottages for tea and cakes; low tides that leave
mirrors in the sand where you can step on the sky.

# Returning

On the first anniversary
of my mother's death, my father
drove into the desert alone, past
ancient adobe walls of San Xavier,
deep into the Santa Cruz valley
in search of the last campsite
                    they shared.

I feared he would not return.
I feared he might become a part
of that desert like the dry, hollow
remains of fallen Saguaros.
I feared they might find him
in a shallow grave of grief
with only memories of my mother
                    for a headstone.

Yet, upon his return he sang
the praise of days among coyotes
and sage hens where he found
that same sharp slant of foothills,
that dry wash of forgiving ground.
There, he placed two chairs near
a campfire and in every snap and pop
of those dried bones of mesquite—
              heard my mother's laugh.

# Sidewalk Table

We sit across the table from each other,
as friends do.
Men, not young, but too young to be old.
We talk of morning's warm sunshine,
cold ocean waters.
Coffee steams in heavy white mugs.
*My father died last week,* he says.

The words hang above the table
between us. Silence
scrutinizes each syllable, turns them
over and over.
*He had a picture of Christ on his dresser.*
Street noise fills his hesitation.
*As far back as I can remember, it was there.*

We sit across from each other,
the table small, yet
accepted as the barrier preventing
a comforting touch. Men don't.
We are warriors. We are hunters.
*I was afraid he wouldn't be there—in Heaven.*
*More afraid he would be in hell for eternity.*

Morning slips into afternoon. More coffee,
talk of children and grandchildren,
and things not so pleasant.
We sit across from each other,
never question God's decisions.

# What Can I Say

I wanted to write about Las Vegas.
Something the Chamber of Commerce
can use, post on a sign at the edge of town.

Nothing too gaudy, a simple sign in keeping
with the Vegas image. Maybe a ten story high
neon billboard with a million red, white and blue
lights flashing to the beat of that old American classic,
*You don't know what you've got until you lose it.*

I wanted to write about the dazzle of casino lights;
not the shadowy sidewalk windows of tattoo parlors
where tourists can watch those not sober enough
to realize the finality of such foolishness.

I wanted to write about the excitement of Texas
Holdem' Poker played on purple felt top tables;
not about the pathetic line of losers at the cashier's
window searching for that back-up Visa card.

I wanted to write about the glitz of bare breasted
beauties on the chorus line, their gold spiked
heels and feathered thongs; not about street sluts
and the plethora of pornography that litters
the sidewalks, creeps into the very soul of the city.

I wanted to write about the glamour of downtown
high-rise condos, balconies suspended above The Strip;
not about cracker-box apartments with bars
on the windows, and 20 year-old Toyotas parked
on the dark streets of crime ridden neighborhoods.

I wanted to write about big winners walking
away with bags of casino money; not the struggle
of single mothers working as change girls
and cocktail waitresses, enduring the desert heat,
the humiliation handed out by drunks.

I wanted to write something about Las Vegas.
Something the chamber of commerce can use.
But, you know what they say, *If you can't say
something nice—don't say anything at all.*

## Somewhere in the Night...

a phone rings, like a bird's sorrowful
song of loss. What else could it be
this time of night? Why can't they wait
until morning, a decent hour
after I've had coffee, perused the paper?

It rings again, demanding
as a groom on his wedding night.
Another ring erases every trace
of sleep as sure as someone shaking
my shoulder, unsympathetic of the hour.

The night disappears into the haze
of my waking thoughts. Calls that come
before dawn are like a telegram
from the Department of Defense,
that somber look on your Doctor's face.

The phone cries again for my attention,
persistent as that murder of crows that
gathers in the eucalyptus out back.

I recall my sister listening to a faceless
voice as a winter storm raged:
*There's been a car crash,*
*your son killed, his girlfriend critical.*

And it was a midnight message
eight years ago that revealed my mother
dying. Then, August of this year, that early
AM call confirmed my father's death.

Yet another ring pierces the night,
pulls me back to the present.
I consider answering the bell, like an old
fighter, already beaten, acting out of instinct.

But the veil of sleep has slipped away
and I realize it is not my phone that beckons.
I pull the covers up, find my woman warm
in bed beside me and know, for the moment
at least, my world is as it should be. Yet,
somewhere in the night—a phone still rings.

# Not All Days...

are good days
for the poet.
On a good day
he has an idea
of where
to find words.
He has an idea
of how
to arrange them
so they
enchant,
entice,
enthrall,
say it all.
But often
crafting even
a couplet
is beyond
his reach.
And that
is a hard day
for the poet,
who relies
on words
for his
good days.

# Cadence

Seduced by the sea, by a wind out of the west,
I stand smooth curve of tiller in hand.
A lover's rhythmic cadence rising on the crest

she shudders beneath me, deck awash in our quest.
A belly of white canvas sail I command,
seduced by the sea, by a wind out of the west.

I cling to her, man at earth's bountiful breast,
then rejoice, each thrust of bow grand,
a lover's rhythmic cadence rising on the crest.

She flies, wind across her beam, reaching, pressed
against clouds and empty sky traced in the sand.
Seduced by the sea, by a wind out of the west

I believe her whispered promise, safe harbor's rest,
sails lowered in the blushing beauty of her land.
A lover's rhythmic cadence rising on the crest

spills sailors and Captain into a sea of confessed
desire. There they surrender to her hand,
seduced by the sea, by a wind out of the west,
and a lover's rhythmic cadence rising on the crest.

# Still

The snowcapped Lagunas fill a window.
Sun makes its statement for the day, plays
on peaks, paints bold shadows to the west.
Sharp stone ridges slash those gentle green
slopes folded across the desert floor.

In this room I sense my mother's presence
in those baskets of seashells from Mexico,
in that long procession of carved turtles,
even in the garlic salt that sits on the stove.

It's been two years, but Father refuses
to change a thing. I remain quiet,
know this decision not mine to make.
So, as distant mountains fill the window
memories of Mother fill this room.

# With the Spring Rain...

   puddles to play in.
She loves jumping in puddles:

random gatherings of liquid magic
   filling the dimples and hollows,
   shiny spots in a parking lot,
   on a playground,
along the edges of old sidewalks.

She loves jumping in puddles:

those mirrors of the world,
   small pieces of sky at her feet,
   blues and blacks and grays
as still as a photograph
         —until she jumps.

## The House I Left Behind

Only the pitch of that moss covered
roof was more precarious than living
in that house with her. The walls
painted with questions the color
of doubt and suspicion; the carpet
always snooping around, not satisfied
I'd wiped my feet before entering.

Mornings, the aroma of a waking
day wafted through the house:
bacon and eggs, toast with jam,
fresh brewed coffee. Yet, I ate alone.

During those dark decades tears fell
furious as wind driven rain,
left stains on her pillow, clouded
my days with gray uncertainty.

My daughter's room, draped in pink,
littered with teddy bears, a plastic
tea party set, offered a sanctuary
of sorts where we paged through
*Winnie the Pooh*, or *Oswald's New Shoes*.
I could see her mother in those big
brown eyes, but couldn't see staying,
couldn't bring myself to leave.

In spring, tulip bulbs burst
with new life around the back porch.
Blackberry bushes and bull thistles
consumed the vacant lot next door,
offered no apologies. And I
spent more time in the vegetable
garden than in that house.

That house I left behind never was
mine. I only sought shelter beneath
her cedar shingles where I watched
and waited for the world to catch up
to my dreams. Watched and waited
as the paint peeled, the roof leaked,
the pipes froze, and I made decisions
about things I couldn't comprehend.

Truth never lived in the house I left behind:
not in the kitchen, nor the hallway, or beyond
the bay window that overlooked the river.
And in the bedroom, we both shivered
in the cold beneath our quilt of lies.

# Powder Monkey

There was one thing Winne Dee would
remember until the last days of her 92nd year:
the color of Roy King's eyes.

They were a blue not found in nature; not in
those slices of sky between the constantly
changing clouds over the Kansas prairie;
not in the depths of a mountain lake nestled
in a wood of pine and alder. It was as if
God had created that hue just for Roy.

There was something else she could not forget:
a Friday in the spring of '32. But only Roy
knew for sure what happened that day.

There was that instant when he knew
all those years of care and caution;
the reverent way he handled dynamite;
the leather harness used to swing him over
the edge, where he crawled across that sheer
rock face to practice his deadly trade
—meant nothing.

there was that instant when he knew
that his wife's prayers, offered up even
before pneumatic drills hammered holes
in gray granite; before twisted coils of fuse
found their place webbed across the face
of a canyon wall—meant nothing.

There was that instant when he knew
he'd never again see the Rockies cloaked
in winter snow, stark against a brilliant blue sky;
feel the oppressive heat of a Kansas wheat field,
or the cool meadow grass of Trout Creek Pass.

There was that instant when he knew
his luck had run out; not like that time
on the Royal Gorge Bridge back in '29.

There was that instant when he knew
the hard times were over for good. No more
12-hour days and raw fingers from clinging
to ragged rock; no more borrowing against
next weeks wages at the company store.

There was that instant when he knew
he would never again hear the screen door slam,
son and daughter home from school, faces bright
with the wonder of life.
There was that instant when he knew
he'd never again see the loving eyes of his wife.

Later, the Company sent his family a final check:
a week's pay minus the four hours he missed
that last day. They kept another three dollars
for the safety gear he never returned.
Of course, they sent a note saying he was
a good man and would be missed, but could she
and the children please be out of the company
house by Monday. The new powder monkey
would need a place to stay.

There is that instant when man becomes memory:
*Roy King*
*1890 - 1932*
*Beloved Husband and Father.*

# Indian Country

I am the mountain —
Where the wind lives with the black bear
in the fetor of a dark cave, and a brooding
sky dances with tribal spirits.
Where the moon is an old scar of light
feeding off remnants of the yellow oracle,
the God of day, who questions your soul
and flings darkness against red stars.
Where rain clouds scowl and hold back like a virgin,
thunder curses the darkness, and lightning's bliss
scorches words offered in pray and song.

I am the foothills —
Where the backbone of the earth, red rock ridges
and blue shadow shapes, stretch for eternity.
Where ragged days bleed into the past
and smoke fires carry spirits into tomorrow.
Where the black curse of death
is stacked on burial alters, covered in skins
of bear and cougar, offered to the Gods,
devoured by scavengers and time.

I am the desert —
Where the heat of sun scared sands explodes at dawn,
snakes writhe and coil and eat their young,
creeks lie dead waiting for a dance to bring rain
that gluts and rips the earth.
Where old men who ran with the wolf now walk
with women, ancient circles of song live only in lore,
naked children cry at their mother's empty breast.

I am Indian Country—
Where warriors fought the future, prayed to the past,
cultures eradicated, the white man truly unjust.
I am Indian Country, mere memories in the dust.

168

# Lovers and Pinecones

I see young women smile and walk,
their long legs stretching a fast gait,
arms and hips swinging
to an unannounced cadence.

I see young women smile
in the park, suckle their babies,
unaware of those who stare.

Young women always smile.
Is the pleasure of being beautiful,
that joy of youth impossible
to conceal, like the quiver
of aspen in a spring breeze?

What do they say to each other
behind those shy smiles?
What do women speak of
when they are in pairs
where men cannot hear?

Do they talk of lovers, men
they have collected, filed away
in the dark drawer of memory
like a child who gathers pinecones
in the forest, only to hide them
in a shoe box under her bed?

## Independence

When I was a boy
my father would not talk about his war.
Yet, he could not forget,
it would not stay on the battlefield.

It returned in pre-dawn hours
when sleep eluded him,
in quiet moments at the park
as children played on the merry-go-round.

Today we celebrate our independence.
Independence won in a war waged
a century and a half before my father's war.
The first fight our nation faced for freedom.

I wonder if those early patriots spoke
of their battles when they returned, heroes
whose victory forged independence
from the fires of tyranny?

Did they speak of Lexington and Concord,
*The shot that was heard around the world,*
battlegrounds immersed in bravery and bloodshed,
of soldiers fallen in freshly plowed fields, dead?

Maybe they mentioned Bunker Hill
or Bennington, Charleston or Yorktown.
Or maybe they were silent,
tended to their wounds, buried their dead,
believing the war over, all had been said.

We celebrate our independence today.
But let us not forget the price those patriots paid.
This country's independence won with the blood
of hundreds of good men.
A sacrifice thought never to be asked again.

But the cost of freedom has always been blood
and more blood. Little wonder Old Glory
so boldly carries broad stripes of red.

Today we celebrate our independence,
salute those who first fought
for our freedom and those who followed,
giving their lives so we may say
what's on our mind, fly our flag,
worship God as we choose.
There are men and women here today
who know the price, the sacrifice.

And there are men and women in Washington
willing to pay in full with someone else's life.
Not every war is a war that should be fought.
Not every battle is about liberty and justice
for all. But a soldier's blood flows
just as red, mothers cry just as long
when sons and daughters are gone.

Today we celebrate our independence
and thank God
a few brave men had a vision
of how great this nation could be.
They fought and died, for you, for me,
for independence.

Today we celebrate.

## Sestina to My Daughter
## and My Daughter's Daughter

My daughter was born in the morning,
following the sun into my heart
where I could not tell one from the other;
where love, saved and hidden away
for months could now be set free.
She, mere minutes old when I knew

what every father before me knew;
what every sunrise means to the morning
sky; why men wage war to be free.
Then, in what seemed like a heart-
beat, the school bus pulled away
that first day destined for the other

side of the world, or the other
end of the galaxy, for all I knew.
For years my child took me away
from the everyday with her morning
hug. But I always sensed the heart-
ache close by, when she would be free

to fly. An angel on silver wings, free
to find her own way, taste the other
side of a rainbow, touch another heart,
chase the sun. And just as I knew
roses would be wet with morning
dew, a Prince swept my child away.

Then, above the stars, shying away
from her vows, she longed to be set free,
to take wing, a white dove in morning
air. If only she hadn't seen the other
faces of love, if only she knew
angels too quickly give their heart,

believing that melody of a heart's
song. So my child turned away
from him, became a woman who knew
her every breath, every thought, free.
Now, with that freedom, made the other
choice to fulfill the late morning

of her life, birthing another free heart.
And I knew she would be to me, like the other
morning child who first carried my heart away.

# Warm Water

the sea falls away    surging
drawn by the moon    driven
by the wind    beckoning
whispering my name

again and again I return
where afternoon sun paints
the waves    gulls screech
cobbles rattle in the surf

beyond the waves    liquid
shadows flash    rainbows
dance through the mist
of dolphin's breath

pelicans drift on wing
single file    never straight
I stare into the white abyss
of afternoon    searching

for answers along these shores
where billowed sails run before
the wind    silent    unnoticed
like the years of my life

# Tuesday in Tucson

My father and I sit in white plastic chairs
on his porch, sun low in a soft desert sky.
Last year, from here, we could see dusty
brown mountains rimming the horizon,
barren faces mimicking moonscapes
photographed by astronauts.

But now, we are unable to see beyond
faux wood siding and composition roofing,
a mobile home so near we feel heat
reflected off its cream colored length.
Unlike those far off reminders of lunar
topography, that bleak aluminum box rings
with life, annoying proof we are not alone.

Reluctant to accept change, even while
it sits sweltering some thirty feet away,
we drag our chairs to the end of the porch
where a glimpse of that dusty
mountain range can still be seen.

My father speaks without looking at me,
eyes focused on the past, *Your mother and I
used to sit out here every night.* I say nothing,
know we cannot go back, know I must tell him
I'm leaving for home on Wednesday.

# Then and Now

There was a time when I had a big house,
two cars, a boat, 2.3 kids and a Jack Russell
terrier in the back yard. There was soccer
and little league, BMX , ballet and the PTA.
Finally, the kids grew up and moved out.
My wife suggested I do the same.

So, I took an apartment at the beach, near
the sand so I could hear the surf at night,
wander the shore by day. But, it had been decades
since I last lived in a communal setting and I had
forgotten about the intimacies of apartment life.

Next door, an alcoholic and his 14-year-old son
shout at each other late into the night. The old
man moans about his latest girlfriend leaving.
His son says he didn't like her anyway, hopes
she never comes back, and it starts all over.

Upstairs, a guy with a bullhorn voice talks
on the phone until three AM, unless he's entertaining
guests. They usually don't arrive until about 11,
never leave before four. He takes their shoes,
passes out clogs. They dance on the balcony,
play shuffle board in the kitchen.

Newly weds on the other side start earlier.
Their bed bangs the wall for what seems
an eternity, then, a chorus of *Oh Gods*, and I
think, *Thank God*. But soon, it begins again.
So I step outside for some fresh air and quiet.

That kid in the studio over the garage spends
every waking hour sitting in his open window
talking on his cell phone, You'd never guess by his
tattoos and body piercings, his sideways hat, and
pants hanging half way down his butt, that he is a master
linguist. He speaks in sentences composed entirely
of four letter words. Never before have I heard f--k
used as a noun, verb, pronoun, adjective, adverb
and preposition—in the same sentence.

So I guess apartment living hasn't changed much
since the sixties. I remember guys falling down drunk
on Red Mountain wine; Dick Dale's guitar music
screaming from a record player; doing the surfer's stomp,
huarache sandals slapping the linoleum; and young,
blond, beach bunnies everywhere.

Hey, I can still do this. I think there's a pair of sandals
under the bed. I'll run out and get a jug of Red Mountain,
turn up the stereo 'til the windows shake. Then all I need
are a few.... young.... blond.... beach bunnies........
Hmmmm....wonder if it's too late to get into a game
of checkers at the senior center?

# Father

Father told me once
his early days were lost beyond recall.
So in his eighty-seventh year he returned
to that Kansas farm town of his youth.
There, the whisper of wheat fields,
the creak of old barns held together
with nothing more than memories of better times,
the dead silence of his father's headstone
spoke to him. He found his childhood home
still standing, smaller than he remembered;
the schoolhouse where he carved his name
on the front steps seven decades ago,
that same one room schoolhouse
where he fell in love with his third grade teacher;
and down the road the Olsen Farm
where he worked summer harvests.
Those cherished remnants of his past
rekindled stories shared around the dinner table.
Then, on a late August day, with many tales
still untold, he too became a memory
that lives within me like an unwritten poem.

# Soleri Windbell

The afternoon sun sits low,
tosses down more shade than light.
That first sigh of evening breeze
flutters the pages of your book.
A Soleri Windbell that hovers
above the porch tolls.
The bronze sail that dangles
from the clapper tugs and twirls
with each breath of wind.
The phone rings: your daughter.
Another crisis that demands
parental wisdom. *Tell him*
*you're never going to be*
*a couple again,* you say.
The Windbell tolls
as if to underscore your dictum.
*Tell him he should move back*
*to Oregon, live with that friend*
*of his in Corvallis. Tell him*
*three months of flowers, showing up*
*with pizza doesn't make up*
*for three years of drugs, temper*
*tantrums and trashing your place.*
There is silence on the other end.
The Windbell tolls again.
Its rich ring so unlike that clink
of your neighbor's glass wind chime.
And see how the weather has colored
the bronze: brilliant reds that rival
a November sunset; shimmering
shades of turquoise and emerald.
You snap your phone shut.
*Tell him, tell him*, you say,
your words carried away
on the afternoon breeze.

## Dinner

She brings raspberries and almonds
with rosemary, organic tomatoes
red as a November sunset, fresh salmon
caught wild in cold Atlantic waters.

In my kitchen she works culinary magic
with grilling pan and a square bottle
of olive oil. I stand behind her at the stove
with the pretense of helping,
nibble her nape, search out her ear lobe.

Dinner, a gourmet treat.
There is no question about dessert.

# Walking the Dogs

Early January the evening air is cool;
sun the color of fresh squeezed lemonade;
soil beneath our feet damp from last night's rain.

Our dogs scurry about. The old female limps
as she tries to keep up with the younger male.
They investigate every bush in search of lizards,

the occasional rabbit. Across the highway
the sea glistens in the sun's waning light.
We watch the sky redden, the horizon swallow

those last remnants of day. The dogs bark,
chase each other in play. The air is cold now,
night mere minutes away. My love

pulls her sweatshirt hood around her face,
reminds me of Little Red Riding Hood.
Oh, how I want to be the Big Bad Wolf.

## March Wind

You sit under your favorite
wind-swept tree, its broken shadow
lying in the sand, search the horizon
for whale spouts. (It's that time of year.)
Down the beach gulls screech, fight
for bread crumbs an old man tosses
into the sky. A cold wind nips your neck,
the same chill that swept over you
when a court clerk stamped
a case number on your divorce papers.

# Sans Underwear

As we cross the church parking lot
she casually comments,
*I'm not wearing underwear.*
I fall a few steps behind,
check for those telltale panty lines.
None, that I can see.
I could search for those small ridges,
run my hand over her bottom,
but we are in the sanctuary now.
Too many people around for me
to fondle my lady. Announcements
are made. I hear only, *I'm not wearing
underwear.* There is prayer, a song,
I hear only, *I'm not wearing underwear.*
We're in the house of God
and all I can think of is taking a peek
under her dress. Maybe drop something
on the floor. No, too school-boyish.
There is more prayer and songs
and the image of *no underwear*
begins to fade and I suspect
it was a tease. But, after the service,
at home, she looks me straight in the eyes,
smiles and peels off her dress.
There is shock, there is joy, there is laughter.
There is no underwear.

# Father's Final Words

So this is what it all comes down to.
The three of us, knee deep in the sea,
hold hands like school children
crossing the street. Small, indifferent
waves break around us, their white froth
mimics the clouds above. My sister
offers up words I rarely hear from her,
addressing God as if she knows Him.

I dip my hand into Father's ashes.
He slips between my fingers, weightless
as an evening breeze off the Pacific;
that same somber tone of ash spewed forth
from Vesuvius. But only we three
will remember this day, this scattering
of memories, this mixing of tears
and ash and ocean, this goodbye.

So this is what it all comes down to.
Eight pounds of cremains swirl
in the ebb tide and we listen to the sea
for Father's final words.

## Old Man at the Diner

His tee-shirt hangs loose from bony shoulders.
It reminds me of my father, how some things
just slip away: once muscled arms and chest,
sag, rounded with the weight of years.
The old man across from me eats slowly.
(Still an hour until Jeopardy.)
Perched on his nose, bifocals smudged
with fingerprints; a dog-eared paperback
in front of him, not a page turned
the entire meal. Failing light falls through
a window, catches a wisp of hair
on his slick pate, the loneliness in his eyes.
I think how different we are. Then, at home,
I'm surprised by my reflection in the mirror.

# The Citrus Grove

There is a small hill behind our house.
where we planted citrus trees.
Our first crop was meager:
grapefruit the size of lemons,
navel oranges masquerading as tangerines.
But, the blood oranges, when sliced open,
were like setting suns scattered atop
the kitchen counter. Soon the grove
was more than we could manage:
the pruning, spraying, picking.
So, we solicited help with the trees.
A man named Raul showed up:
tall, muscled, dark from days in the sun.
He said he knew citrus, understood
their blossoms, sympathized
with those curling leaves, would settle
for nothing less than the best bounty.
On his battered Ford truck he carried
ladders for the harvest; in the cab,
an old suitcase held everything else
he owned. That first season he appeared
each morning just before the sun.
My wife took him coffee.
A kind gesture I thought. But then,
coffee became breakfast. I noticed
Raul was now clean shaven every day.
My wife had a renewed interest in citrus.
*Just something to keep me busy*, she said.
> Now, when my neighbors inquire of her
> whereabouts I tell them, *...a world cruise*
> *with her sister.* Later I will explain,
> *She met a man in Madrid.*
> There is a hill behind our house where we
> planted citrus trees. This year, in a small plot
> of freshly turned earth, there are two new trees.

## Finding Raul

Visceral visions pillage your mind,
usher you into this ghoulish grove.
Your shovel slices wet soil
like a surgeon's scalpel.
The handle creaks
with the weight of its burden.
Grotesque ground dissected,
nightmares grin from a silent mouth.
The blade pierces earth again & again.
She shrieks. Her soil bleeds.
Humanity is unearthed: extremities,
half a face, a thumb hitching a ride.
Ebony, the shade of night, the color
of death, fills empty eye sockets.
Blood, no longer red, nor fluid,
is of little use to amputated souls.
A haunting stench slithers
from the depths of this murderous void.
Air begins to chill, coyotes howl,
the moon flickers behind tattered clouds.
The unveiling terminates with prayer.
If only there was a virgin to sacrifice.

      At sunrise you confront Patron, inquire
      of your brother Raul, ignore the lies.
      Later, as the sun dies, haunts the horizon,
      you stash a few boxes in the citrus cooler.
      On each a note that instructs:
      *Perishable, keep refrigerated.*

# Chest Pain

The technician smears a warm jell
on your chest, probes in slow circles.
An image jumps across the screen
erratic as a rabbit's escape route.
You never expected heart problems.
But then, you never expected divorce
after forty years of marriage, or dreamed
you'd find the love of your life at sixty-eight.

An attractive Asian woman enters the room.
White lab coat. A stethoscope draped
around her neck, more like jewelry
than a medical instrument.
She appears to be, maybe nineteen-years-old.
That's about right though. Those Paramedics
in the ambulance looked all of fourteen.

She goes into her spiel, compares the human heart
to a house. An aging heart to an old house:
poor electrical wiring, crumbling foundation,
collapsing walls. You check the I.D. tag
on her breast pocket, try to determine
if she is a Doctor or a General Contractor.

The last time your heart ached like this
was grade school, when Cheryl Benson
said she liked Tommy Wilson better.

Your Doctor orders more tests.
It's not about *puppy love,* this time.

# The Color of Blood

The morning paper lies
on the table, still sequestered
by a red rubber band,
soggy as poorly prepared French toast.
Nobody expected rain last night.
A story on page seven reads so matter-of-fact,
succinct as a headstone:

>  *San Diego photographer*
>  *mauled, eaten by a grizzly.*

I can't help but wonder who he left behind.
In his last minutes, before being gutted
like a fresh caught salmon, did he call out
their names, or turn to his God?

And what of the bear:
600 pounds of muscle and rage,
teeth the size of steak knives,
straight razors for claws.

It must have been her cubs foraging
in the berries. We will do anything
to protect our young. She couldn't
know he only wanted pictures:
she the star, he the paparazzi.

When park officials shot and killed her
some thought it an injustice. Others saw
it only as the color of blood on the snow.

## Terra Mar

I barely set foot on the sand when that pungent odor of rotting
seaweed engulfs me, sweeps me away like a rogue wave back
to my childhood where every day smelled of decaying kelp and
Coppertone sun tan lotion, the legacy of all who lived in a
Southern California beach town, those small communities
clinging to PCH like life itself depended on it, towns scattered
along that ribbon of asphalt like a string of pearls draped around
the slender neck of the Southern California coast, Manhattan,
Redondo and Palos Verdes, Belmont Shores, Huntington, San
Clemente and Oceanside, Del Mar, La Jolla and PB, where life
taught you respect for the ocean, her many moods, that sway of
the moon, earth's rotation, whitecaps born of a far off storm,
spindrift dancing in the sky, unseen currents stirred by Neptune's
scepter, and in those early years you went with questions,
expected to find answers in bits of broken shells, that mystical
glide of pelicans, a tangle of seaweed strewn on the sand, and you
listened to her voice late at night, at times angry with the distant
thunder of breakers, or nearly silent, so subdued you dressed and
went down to the shore to quell your fears that somehow those
dark waters had evaporated into the shadowy night, spilled over
the horizon. But, for those who love her, the sea is always there.

# Musings of the Tin Man

What was it Mother said:
never play near a recycling center
or insult a man carrying a can opener.

It's not like life was easy before WD40,
what with all that salt they toss across
the yellow brick road every winter.

And my uncle talks of times
he and my aunt Lizzy vacationed
at the shore, how he rubbed her down
with 30 weight Pennzoil, polished
her back side with a Brillo pad.

Yet, later in life when the rust
refused to be rebuffed
she had zerk fittings installed.

And of course my grandfather's
tales of his brother the rusty Buick,
my cousins the sardine cans.

Yes, I know, I'm not proud of it,
but you can't choose your relatives.

Now, here I stand caught in the rain,
rust stains swirling around my ankles,
me without an umbrella or KY jelly.

I should have stayed home, enjoyed
a nice warm cup of liquid wrench.
I should have listened to Mother.

## Two-bit Memories

We cruise A&W in hand-me-down cars.
A gallon of gas, a pack of smokes—25 cents.
AM radios spill Chuck Berry and Elvis
into the parking lot where carhops
scurry between Chevys and Fords
festooned with flipper hubcaps, chrome
tipped duals and Mickey Mouse whitewalls.

We comb our hair constantly, duck tails
and flat tops, pompadours that defy gravity.
The sweet scent of Brylcream and Butchwax
mingles with the stale smell of cigarettes.
We wear tight white tee shirts, lean muscled
arms draped out the window, a pack of Luckys
rolled in the sleeve, only the wish of a tattoo.

We roam city streets, always on the move
like sharks searching for prey, praying
we'll run into those two girls in that
white Corvair: the cute blond, her chubby
redheaded friend whose name none of us
can remember. Or that chick who speeds
around town in her daddy's Dodge,
willing to invite boys into the back seat.

We pile on the miles, smoke until the pack
is empty, never give it a second thought.
We are children of the *good times:*
Vietnam still buried deep in the evening news;
that open window above a grassy knoll in Dallas,
the crowded kitchen in the Ambassador hotel,
Martin's final *I have a dream*, somewhere in the future.
And, everything we want only costs a quarter.

# The Nature of Love

I recall those hours
we first roamed free
in the valleys,
across the plateaus
of our bodies.
How we pushed
against each other
like continental plates
that birth earthquakes
and tsunamis.

I can still hear
those small sounds
that flew
from your mouth
like hummingbirds
and hovered
in candlelit bedroom air,
spirits of our love affair.

# Extraction

The dog and I sit on the porch.
He is stretched out, taking it easy,
as if he put in a hard day at the office.
For me the pain medicine isn't working,
so I pop another. My body knows,
down to the very marrow of my bones,
that a small piece of the whole is missing.
The blood is a protest, my mouth in mourning.
The pain relief is too subtle. I pop another
pill, drift back to the morning's ordeal.

The dentist puts her knee on my chest
like a Narc who has just taken down a junkie.
Small grunts leak from behind her mask.
Beads of sweat dot her forehead.
I wonder if she regrets choosing
dental school over Harvard Law.
On the tray next to my chair
every stainless steel instrument
found in a B movie torture chamber.
*You will feel nothing,* she says. The pressure,
like a small truck running over your jaw,
is normal. That cracking sound, similar
to a glacier calving, is normal.
*You will feel nothing*, she says.
Her assistant holds my shoulders
against the chair. The Dentist has
both knees on my chest now. Then,
my tooth, rooted like a white oak
for six decades, finally surrenders.

Back on the porch, afternoon sun
warms my face. An ocean breeze
rattles fronds on my neighbor's palm tree
and the pain medicine has kicked in
like a runaway locomotive.
An egret wings its way in the distance
Janis Joplin astride its back; my dog
levitates up and over the porch rail,
disappears in a flash of light;
the potted geraniums sing
*Lucy in the Sky With Diamonds.*
As promised, I feel nothing.
I pop another pain pill—just to be sure.

## Apps

I don't own a smart phone.
Don't have an app
to help me find a place to eat
then post a picture
of my meal on Face Book.
Don't have an app that tells me
the freeway is gridlock
commuters on the brink of road rage,
their Starbucks Mocha *whatever*
gone cold in biodegradable cups,
some considering suicide by collision.
Don't have an app that reveals
how far I've walked or exactly
where I am on that worldwide grid
of latitude and longitude.
Don't have an app that allows me
to watch movies on a four inch screen,
or one that lets me kill space aliens
while I wait for a green light.
And because I don't own a smart phone,
some suggest I live in a cave. Maybe.
But in my cave: a novel or two,
a stack of poetry books, inked words
emblazoned on real paper waiting
for that slow turn of the page.
And in my cave: my thoughts,
my imagination. No apps necessary.

## Heaven's Lights

I walked to the edge of the earth
in search of sunset. Yet the sun
simply faded from sight, cloistered
in clouds clinging to the horizon.

I watched daylight slip away
in an unceremonious play
of blue into gray into black,
with no trace of a crimson sky.

But, as I turned toward home,
a full moon shone in ebony air,
there, seemingly born of rooftops
and the leaves of a lone eucalyptus.

And I was unable to look away
from that brilliant display of cold
reflected light, light gifted
to the moon by an unselfish sun.

I mention this only because being apart
is more devastating than a failed sunset.
But seeing your smile again is more glorious
than all those shared lights of heaven.

# Vigilante Gardeners

A woven wooden trellis of roses stands
between us and our neighbor's yard,
a jungle of dandelions and crabgrass,
a constant threat to our potted geraniums,
the chives and basil we water with
the lead free hose, our miniature peach tree
that yields only two or three globes a season.

She is a practicing recluse venturing out only
on Wednesdays to attend mass, receive communion.
So we wait, listen for the rattle of her old Buick
as she leaves for Saint Patrick's, arm ourselves
with spade and sprayer, sneak into her yard,
attack and kill every broadleaf in sight.
Should we get caught, we plan to plead self defense.

# The People

Central Park is an oasis
in a towering concrete and glass
desert that is New York City.
On this September day
the sky is a cloudless umbrella,
a blue hue yet unnamed;
the sidewalks, a frenzy of activity.
Overwhelmed by the park's size
we hire a rickshaw. A young man
from Michigan provides the muscle
and narrative. Yet, my lady is not content
with only seeing the Valentine Garden
or Yoko's apartment above the park.
She questions the young man like a mother
who hasn't talked with her son in years.
He works the park summers, spends winters
volunteering at a medical clinic in India.
Later, my lady reminds me, *It's not the tourist
attractions that make a city—it's the people.*

# New York Heat

I recall the first time
we kissed goodnight
then awoke
in the same bed:
that small hotel room
in Greenwich Village
with its faux fireplace,
red velvet wallpaper
and those ridiculous
steer horns on the wall.
Outside, people scurried
along the sidewalk,
a heated chorus of taxi horns
threatened pedestrians
and echoed down
a tree lined canyon
of old brick façades.
You slid closer.
We found each other
between the sheets.
We missed breakfast,
and lunch. All the while
that window air conditioner
labored to save us
from spontaneous combustion.

# Sunday Ride

When you ride a motorcycle
it's not important the roads you travel
lead to where you are going.

The back road to Laguna Beach
snakes through Silverado Canyon
where clusters of small cabins
cling to hillsides, hidden
by a camouflage of trees and shadow.
You carve your way down the valley,
attack each turn, lean deep, defy gravity
and common sense. Your foot pegs
leave long scars in the pavement.
That staccato rasp of straight pipes
hangs in the air as you dash
through tunnels of shade,
flash across plateaus of sunlight.
Then, just as sudden as death itself,
clouds erase the sky and rain falls.
That double yellow becomes slick
as a used car salesman. Raindrops
sting like gravel tossed from heaven.
You creep into Laguna Beach,
find a Laundromat, strip down
to your boxers. There you stand,
a skinny, shivering seventeen-year-old,
wondering what might happen
should someone come in to do laundry.

## The Afternoon Sidewalk...

is crowded with the usual characters:
tattooed men, old enough to be husbands
& fathers, who roll around town like school boys
on their skateboards; & those women, taut & tan,
determined to hold on to youth; & the others,
already round with age & neglect; & the old men
who sit on concrete benches with their lap dogs
& watch the young girls. Though you are nowhere in sight
this afternoon sidewalk will help me get through the day.
But, without you, how will I survive the night?

# Chairs

The neighbor has a white plastic chair
sitting atop her trash can.
It reminds me of those chairs
my father had on his porch in Tucson:
hard and unforgiving, a blunt blade
of cheap plastic cutting into your back.
The neighbor's chair is unadorned,
plain white. My father's chairs
had Mexican beer logos emblazoned
on them: Tecate, Dos Exes, Corona.
You might say they were branded
the way ranchers brand their cattle
so they can prove ownership.
But we know rustlers don't care
and steal them anyway.
So it was a few years back
when my mother and father wandered
Mexico in that old Dodge truck.
They needed chairs for those evenings
by the campfire and a couple extras
for the occasional guest. So, one day
they stopped at a small cantina
on the outskirts of town, had lunch
and a beer on the patio, then
walked off with half a dozen chairs.
Years later, after my mother's death,
my father sold their place in Tucson
and moved to Nevada. But those chairs
remained on that porch. After all,
you know how risky it is to drive
a herd of stolen cattle across the state line.

# A Morning at Ponto Beach

Pelicans sprawl across a gray collage
of sky, a lazy line unlike those sharp
vees of migrating ducks and geese.
They dip low over the sea, mirrored
in her glassy surface, wing in unison,
then glide—wing, glide—wing, glide.
I wonder if the last in line calls out
the rhythm, the pace, like a coxswain
in a racing shell. I listen, hear only
silence, the occasional surrender
of waves. Now, the pelicans are gone,
disappeared from sight in the time
it took me to write these few lines,
much the way life slips away
while we are busy with something else.

# Running in the Yard

Today, my childhood home
looks much the same as I remember
even though its rough stucco exterior
is a different color and that old acacia,
that dropped yellow blossoms like
a snow storm, is gone. And that jungle
of ivy that consumed the entire corner
of our front lawn is now just a memory.
In the back, a room has been added
where two orange trees stood. A Valencia
and a navel: juice for breakfast,
orange boats for school lunch bags.
The rest of the backyard is that same
patch of grass surrounded by planters
built by my father with homemade bricks.
Yet, it seemed larger when I was a boy
tossing a football or playing with our dog.
I remember my father and me
having footraces in that yard.
I never lost a race and couldn't
understand why he was so slow.
Years later I had a son of my own. We ran
across that same lawn, and I understood.
It's love that makes a father slow.

## 13 rue Paul Albert

The Eiffel Tower blazes like a torch
in these last minutes of a Parisian night.
Our plane touches down as dawn
spills across the French countryside.
We wander the airport, find our way
to the train station and into Paris.
Our apartment, a two-hundred-year-old
building, hugs a cobble-stone street
at the foot of Basilica Sacré-Coeur.
We find a bottle of wine, some fruit
and cheese on the kitchen counter,
compliments of the owner, an artist
who lives on the floor above us.
Sunlight slips through an open window
along with morning sounds of Montmartre,
the smell of warm croissants and strong
coffee from a little café below. We don't
bother to unpack but fumble with buttons
and zippers, litter the floor with clothing,
can't wait to be in love in Paris.

# Monday Morning

I stand at the coffee maker
sleep still heavy in my eyes,
tufts of hair shoot off
toward all points of the compass.
That old Ralph Lauren tee-shirt
she tried to toss a dozen times,
ragged around my neck, hangs
loose off my shoulders. This
breaks my pledge not to wander
the house mornings in only
boxers and a tee-shirt,
my promise to be properly dressed
and groomed before making
my morning appearance.
I hear her footfalls down
the hall: hard soled shoes,
not the padding of naked feet
nor the scuff of sloppy slippers.
She is a vision of morning beauty:
golden ringlets of hair bounce
with the energy of her walk;
a brilliant smile, lip gloss the perfect shade;
her skin vibrant with the secrets
of a Greek goddess; and those eyes
that smiled, no, laughed their way
into my heart. And the wrapping
on the package: a blouse crisp
in virginal white with just the right
number of buttons left undone;
black yoga pants curvy and clinging.
*Good morning*, she says,
her voice music to my ears.
*Any plans for the day*, she asks.
And just like that, I have one.
I want to keep her here
      —and mess her up.

# Demise of a Delphinium

Blossoms litter the ground, leaves
limp as the proverbial wet dishrag.
She has but one choice, ruthless
as it may seem to some: amputate stems
with those pruners she had sharpened
just last week; rip roots, still searching
for that moisture of life, from the earth.
Toss the remains into the greens bin.
There they mingle with others of a similar fate,
later mulched and laid to rest in flowerbeds
at city park playgrounds where children
run and laugh, unaware of death's proximity.

# Another Day at the Office

It's been years since that clutter of desk,
inane babble around the coffee pot
in a windowless tomb of capitalism.

Now, my office is the edge of the sea,
sand warm beneath bare feet. No one
to meet except the incoming tide.

On the sand, remnants of the weekend:
plastic pales, Tupperware tubs
and towering turrets of sandcastles.

I park along the curb where rusted relics
of Detroit iron regurgitate a semi-melodic
ruckus; where tattooed young men

and guys gray with time gather
for our morning ritual in the waves.
Just another day at the office.

## Our Beach

A white belly of moon lingers
in the morning sky, the only
blemish on that pale blue abyss.
A sandpiper's scurry catches my eye,
that race to forage before the next
surge of sea. Above me gulls circle,
call the ocean by name. Sun warms
my shoulders, throws my shadow
down the beach. I hear your voice
in the song of waves, recall that day
you wrote my name in the sand.

# Bridge

I stand atop a new bridge on PCH:
curved steel and concrete arch;
form that flows like the steam below;
the sea that rushes toward it.

That old bridge, really nothing
more than a fancy box culvert,
began to slip into the sea,
sag under the burden of time.
Built back in '27. The same year
Lindbergh soloed to Paris,
*The Jazz Singer* made movie history,
the year my father lost his father.

I imagine those bridge builders
as they labored with the weight
of wooden forms; concrete
mixed on site, one part cement,
two parts sand and aggregate,
an untold amount of sweat.
I can hear them now as they talk
of how the world had changed:
movies that speak, flights across
the Atlantic. Yet, not a word
about my grandfather's death.

So I speak my father's name,
this year of a new bridge,
this year of his death,
so that all might know him
should he pass this way again.

## Garage Sale

An old man, his truck jammed
with other people's castoffs,
haggles over the price of a used surfboard.
His skinny arms hang from a tank top
that hugs his scrawny body like the tees
worn by muscle builders on Venice Beach.
He is one of the serious scavengers,
people who cherish everyone else's junk.
They gather like fruit flies on an overripe
banana, hovering above the scraps of life.

Two women park their rusty Camry
on the wrong side of the street four feet
from the curb. They cruise the driveway
debris without a word, like searching
the ruins of a sunken pirate ship for treasure,
then head off down the street
still in search of that special something
they won't know until they see it.
I don't understand the garage sale mind set,
the need for something you don't need.
Enough of that. I'm on my way to Costco
for capers. I can save a dollar twenty
if I buy a case of ninety-six.

# Writing a Poem for You

I take my coffee to the porch
where I can look out over red tile
rooftops bright in this pale dawn light;
those distant palms, subtle curved lines
in the morning sky. An ocean breeze
turns our flowerbed into a ballet.
Roses bow their heads, French lavender
sways while those yellow blossoms
of a dusty miller look on.
I hear the neighbor's fountain gurgle
in those silent moments between
that far off call of a crow
and a mocking bird's mating song.
I imagined I would write a poem for you,
here on our porch, you watering
flowers, me with pen and paper.
But, I've come to realize it's not where
the poet writes that births a poem,
rather, where the heart is. Mine, my love,
is with you, and you are my poem.

## Your Name

I spend the morning
at our beach
where the sky
is a collage
of confused clouds,
the ocean dappled
with only a thought
of whitecaps,
and a breeze
whispers your name.

# Questions for a Friend

Remember those sweet little waves
in La Jolla Cove right in front
of the tennis club; the security guard
who stood on the beach, waved his arms
in the air like a runaway windmill,
tried to tell us we couldn't surf there?
Do you recall how cold the water was
that summer, how clear; and that rock
ledge along the south shore that would
reach up and snag your fin at low tide;
and when the surf was on the rise,
how we slipped into those deep troughs
between rolling mountains of water;
or those calm days when we surfed
that small left under Scripps pier;
and days we paddled up to Black's
where every wave whispered our name?
Remember how warm the car would be after,
how we basked in its greenhouse effect,
traded tales of waves and wipeouts?
I was in La Jolla today, stopped at the Cove.
Everything was much as I remember it:
swimmers out beyond the buoys; groups
of kayakers gawking at leopard sharks
in the shallows; those insistent swells
marching to shore like an invading army.
Yet, I could not recall exactly where
we all paddled out that summer day,
watched your ashes swirl into the deep.

# The Porch

I bought this house for the porch,
open to the west toward the Pacific.
Ocean breezes curl above the railing
and nudge our windbell into song.
This neighborhood is a bit older
than I'd like. (But then, so am I.)
Evenings I wrap myself in the quiet,
a security blanket worn thin by the years.
This old porch is more than concrete
and wood, brick and mortar.
This porch is a day at the beach,
a night in the desert, an afternoon
in a lover's bed. It's a trip down PCH
in that fast lane of my youth, the first
girl I kissed, that day I filed for divorce.
This porch is the morning my mother
died, our Paris apartment, that train
trip we didn't take to England.
It's the evening my daughter was born,
my first and last day of college,
all those skipped classes in between.
This old porch is our day in Central Park,
Strawberry Fields and Yoko's apartment.
It's Monet's lily pond, my bronzed
baby shoe perched on the bookcase,
our wedding day. This old porch
is that Harley I rode too fast, the first
time I held my granddaughter,
the last time I saw my father.
This old porch is you and me
together in that warm wind of life
flying our love like a kite.

# The Parking Job

Her car teeters on the precipice.
Tires cling as if glued
to the edge of our concrete drive.
I fear gravity & the super moon
may pull her into that quagmire
of sandy soil & ground cover
that creeps along the block wall.
But I wait until after breakfast,
after eggs & fresh cantaloupe,
toast with orange marmalade.
I hold my tongue while coffee
brews, fills the room with
its delicious aroma. Then I speak
in a voice as loving as possible,
*You almost missed the driveway.*
The instant these words fall
from my lips I know I've misspoken
and attempt to turn it into humor
with an uncomfortable laugh.
Later, I call the insurance company,
double our coverage.

## Aloha

We came home with tall tales
of the North Shore of Oahu:
Pipeline, Sunset Beach, Waimea Bay.
Wide eyed surfers believed every word

about the North Shore of Oahu,
seldom surfed in those early days.
Wide eyed surfers believed every word
about that far-away, unattainable Mecca.

Seldom surfed in those early days,
those old style logs not up to the task
in that far-away, unattainable Mecca.
Hawaii beckoned, Barbers Pt. to Diamond Head.

Those old style logs not up to the task
at Pipeline, Sunset Beach, Waimea Bay.
Hawaii beckoned, Barbers Pt. to Diamond Head
and we came home with tall tales.

## Invitation to a Bath Party

There is nothing more enchanting
than a woman fresh from a bath,
skin still damp beneath a wrap
of terrycloth; that faint fragrance
of body wash; those lingering beads
of water between her shoulder blades,
in the small of her back; strands
of wet hair clinging to her nape.

Bring bubble bath if you wish.
You may play with my rubber ducky.

# Alabama Dawn

If I could write music
I'd write a song about an Alabama dawn.
I'd sing about swamp mist,
white as angels wings; morning dew
so soft it surely falls from heaven.

I'd sing about red clay hills
the longleaf pine, coal mines,
summer rain and Gulf Shore shrimp boats.

I'd sing about towns and cities:
Abernathy, Archer and Arlington;
Birmingham, Montgomery and Harper Hill;
Sealy Springs and Selma.

I'd sing about freedom riders,
freedom marchers and freedom fighters
—if I was sure what to say.

I'd sing about the people:
innocent children, the old men
and women who know the truth.

I'd sing about the faces:
brown, black, white, yellow, red;
how they'd all get along
when they heard my song.

I'd sing about the cotton fields,
Rosa Parks' bus ride, drinking
fountains, segregation and integration
—if I was sure what to say.

If I could write music
I'd write a song about an Alabama dawn.

# My Son

Joey—I remember the day we met.
The day I knocked on the door
of that small, friendly house,
looked down into the bright eyes
                    of a little boy.

I remember how you took my hand
and we walked together
through the neighborhood;
how you pulled away, ran ahead,
then turned to see if I had followed.

I remember holding out my arms,
calling your name. You came running
and hugged me around the neck.

I remember the day we met,
that day you held my heart in your hands,
the day I met my son.

## Watching the Last Sunset of the Year
## While Walking the Dogs

Wind blusters down from the north
where foothills veiled in snow
glow under an early evening sun.
The dogs are busy in the brush
doing what dogs do when unleashed.
In the campground across the highway
motor homes and tents perch atop
a bluff overlooking the Pacific.
The sun drops low in the sky,
a glorious display of red and apricot.
Everything in silhouette, dark
against dying embers of another year.
I wonder, *How many more?*
But of course, we never know.
I call the dogs and head home
to love my woman as if it were
our last time—our first time.

About the author:

Clifton King was born in Southern California where he has lived most of his life, with the exception of a sojourn in Oregon to raise a family and fish for steelhead. He now resides in a beach town north of San Diego and is retired from the inconvenience of working for a living. He is an award winning poet whose work has appeared in literary journals, anthologies and online.

*Royale Road Publishing*

20251627R00137

Made in the USA
San Bernardino, CA
03 April 2015